I0472866

Beach

Daze

Illustrations by Skye Heyden

Beach Daze

A salty coloring experience

Published October 2017

Happy Daze Design

ISBN: 978-0-692-94819-4

Copyright © 2017 Skye Heyden

All rights reserved.

No parts of this book may be reproduced, stored in a retrieval system, or transmitted, in any form or by any means (electronical, mechanical, photocopying, recording or otherwise) without the prior written permission from the publisher

Try out some of those awesome colors here!

An ice cold glass of beach daze

will wash your worries away

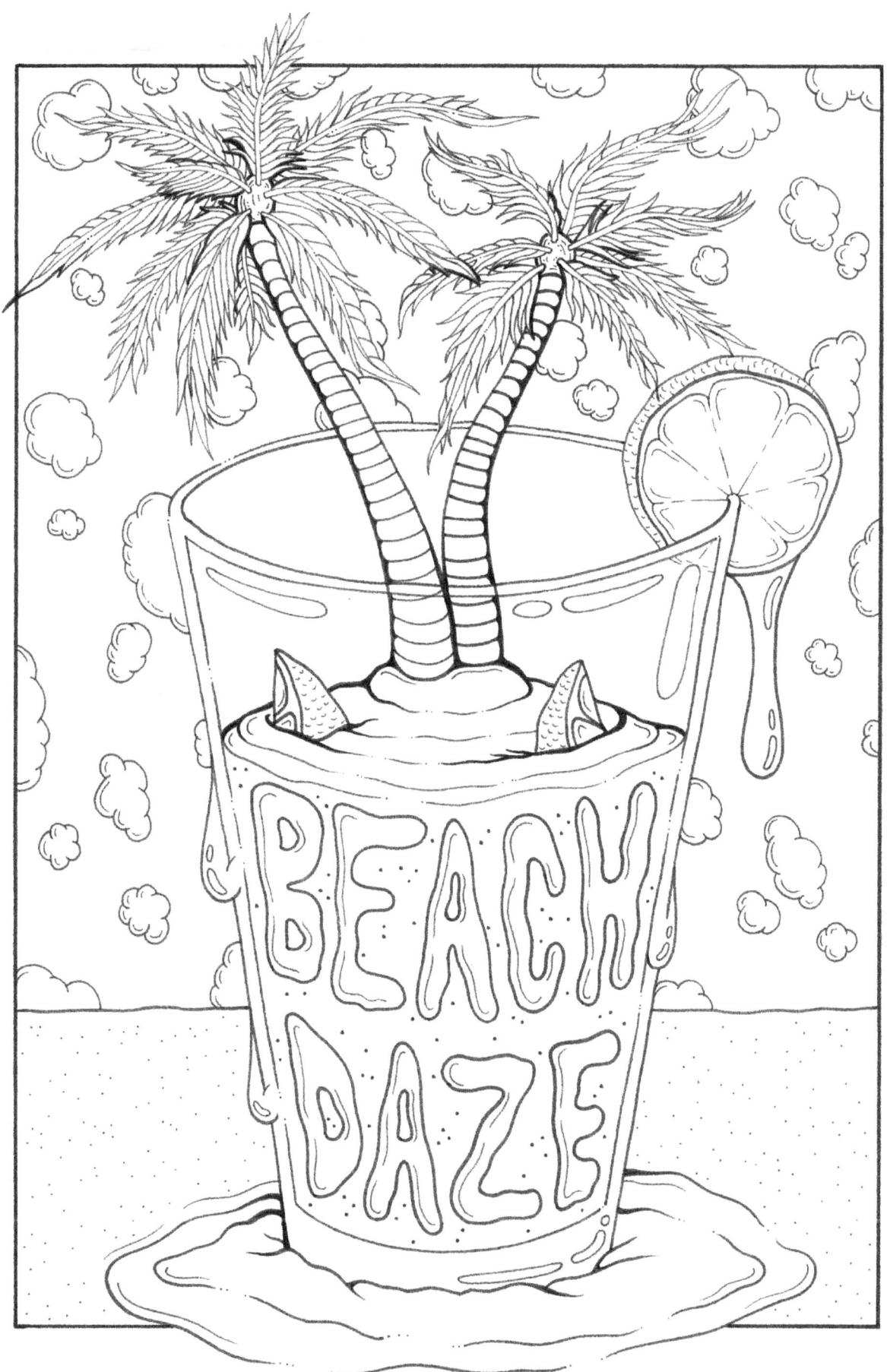

A day in the waves is the best way to play

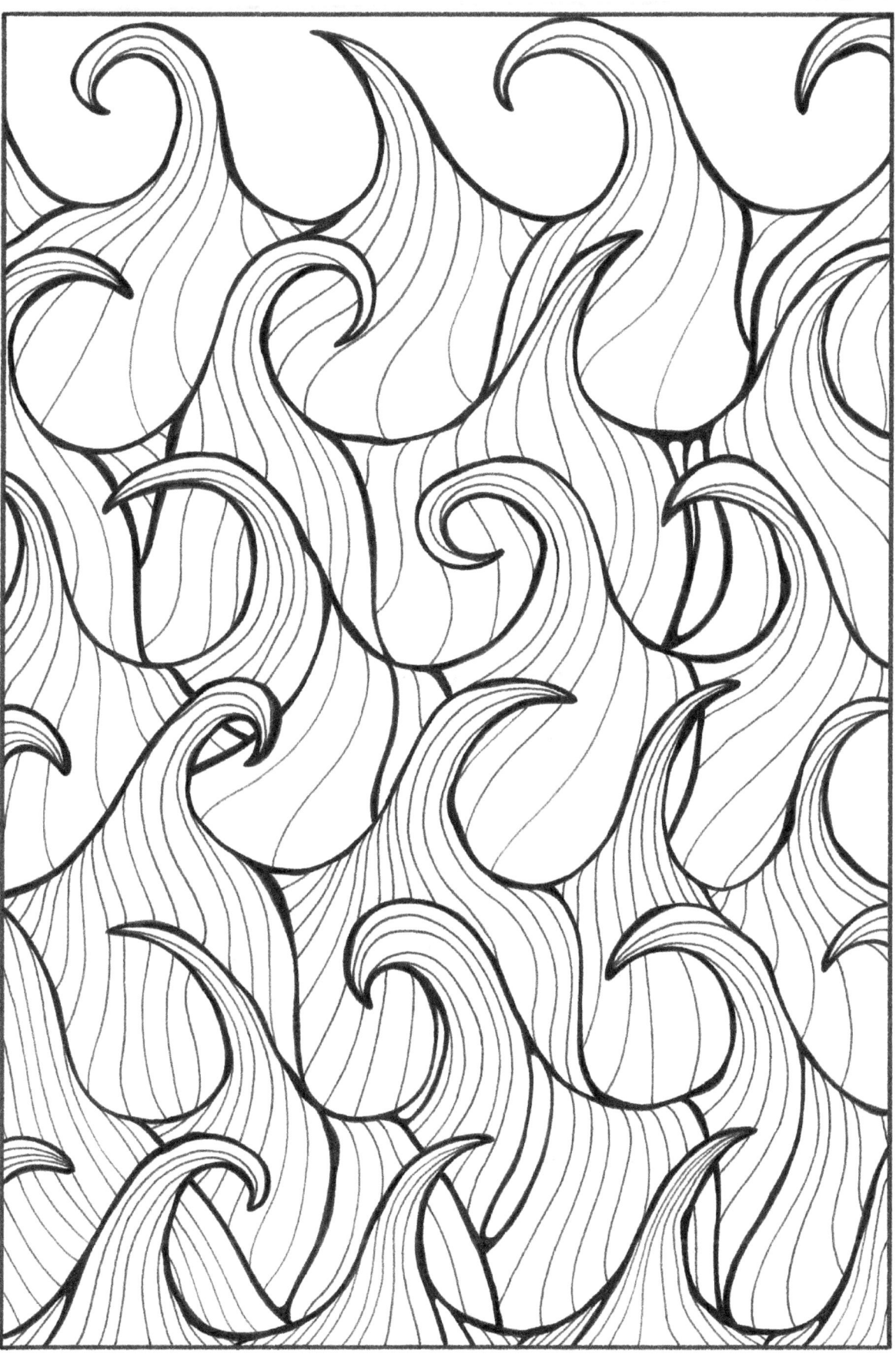

This log rider has the right idea...

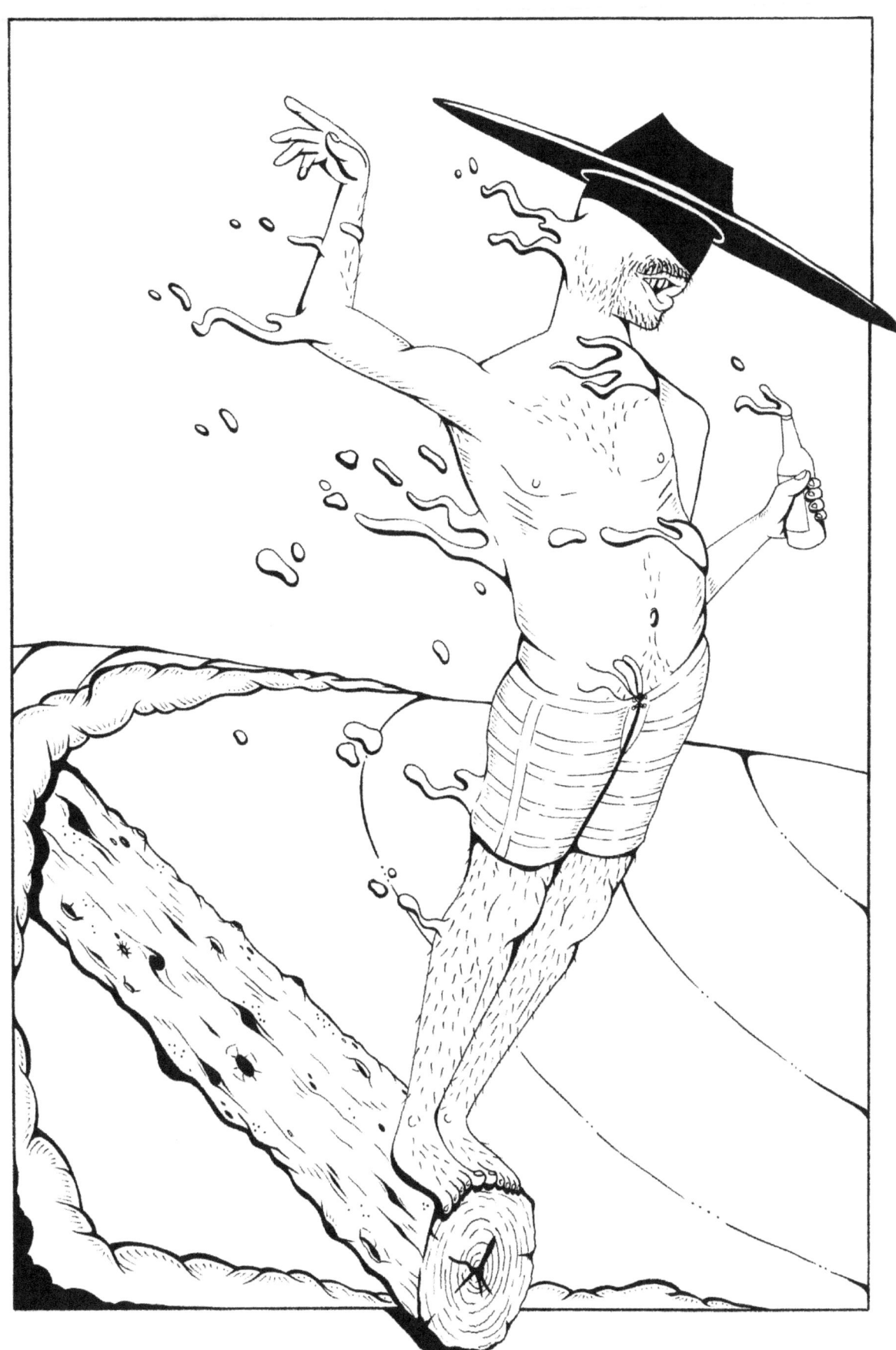

...and after he swam in

He started jammin'

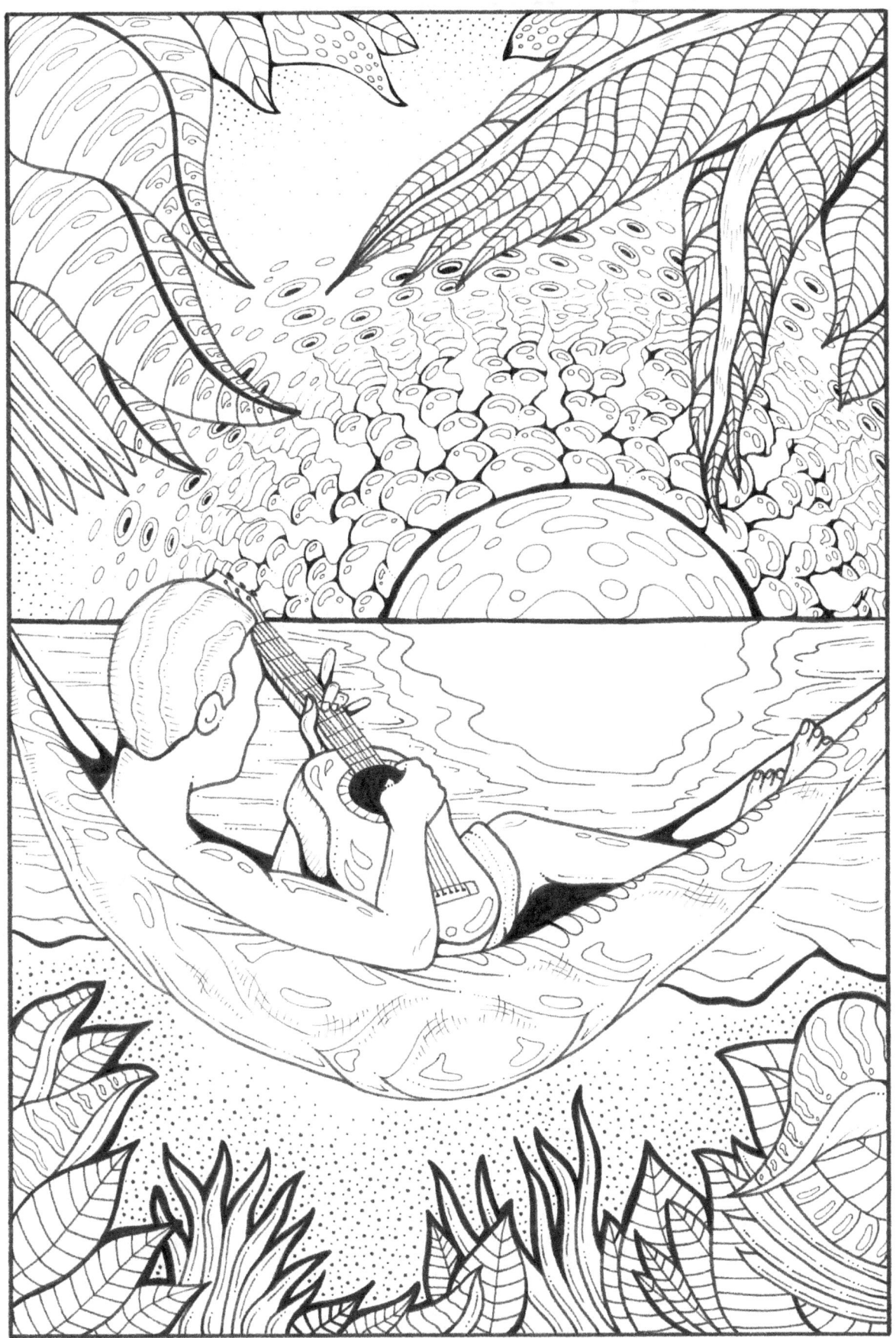

If sharks are circling you

It's probably because they want to be friends

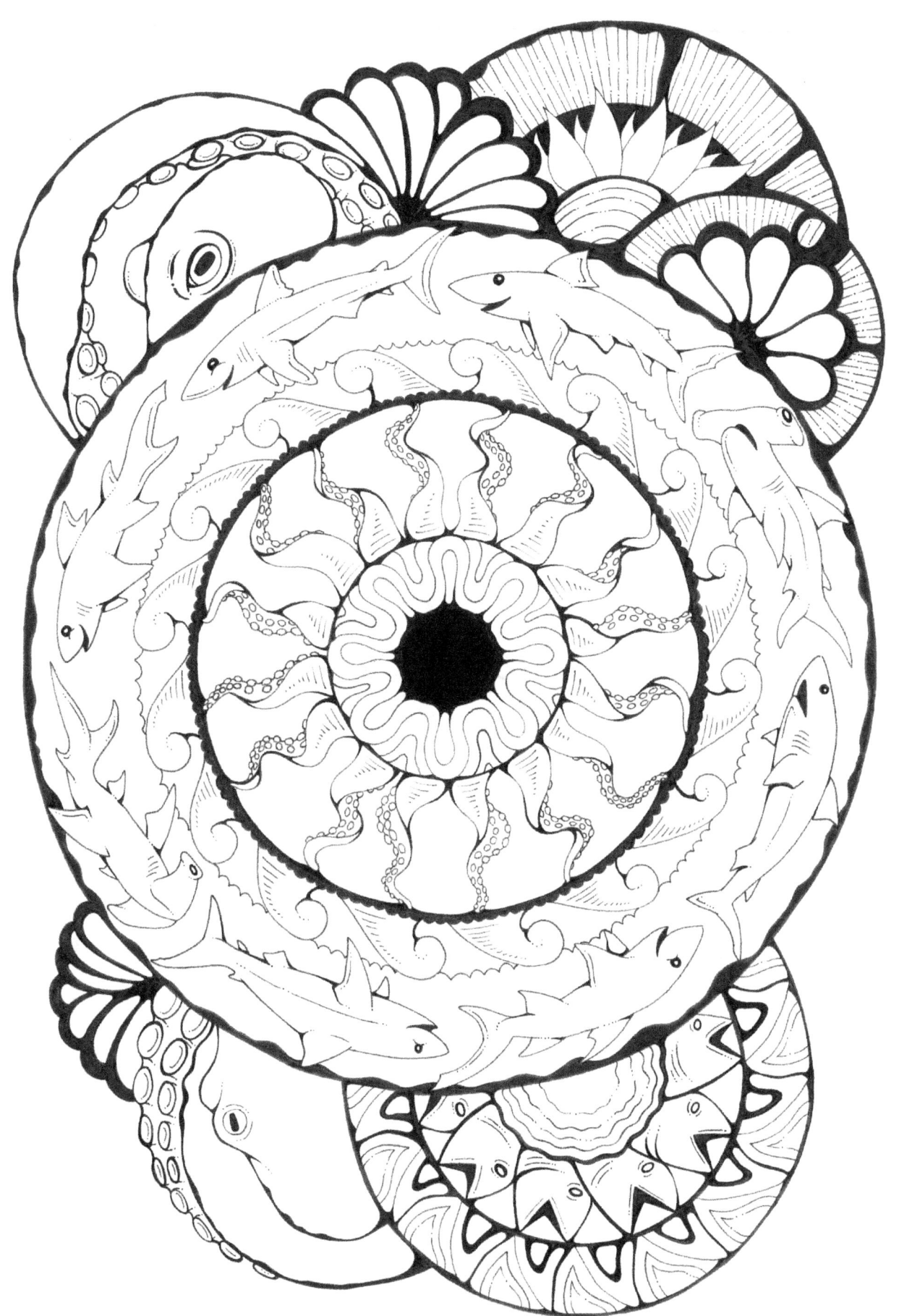

A wonderful sight on this windy night

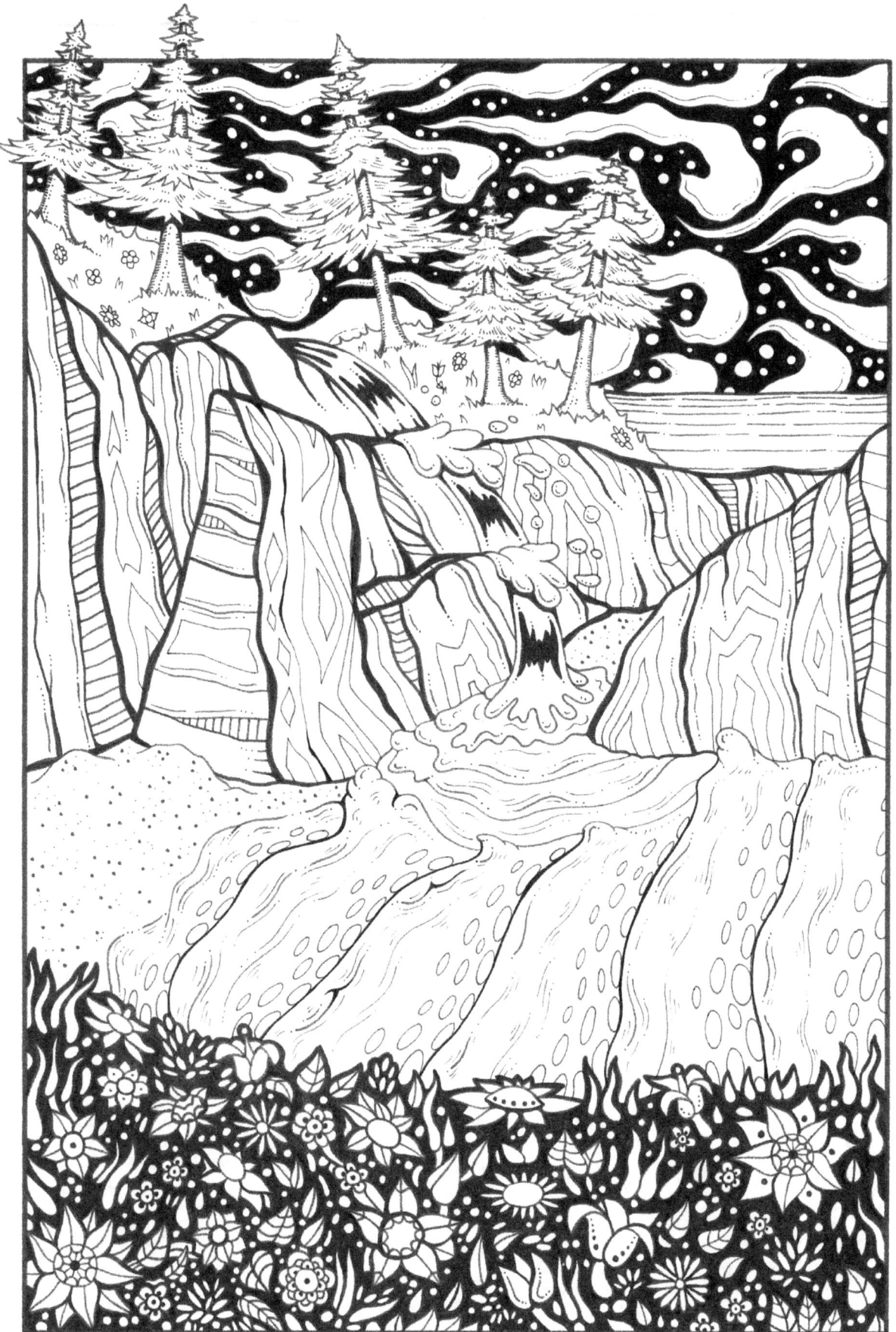

It's a hootenanny!

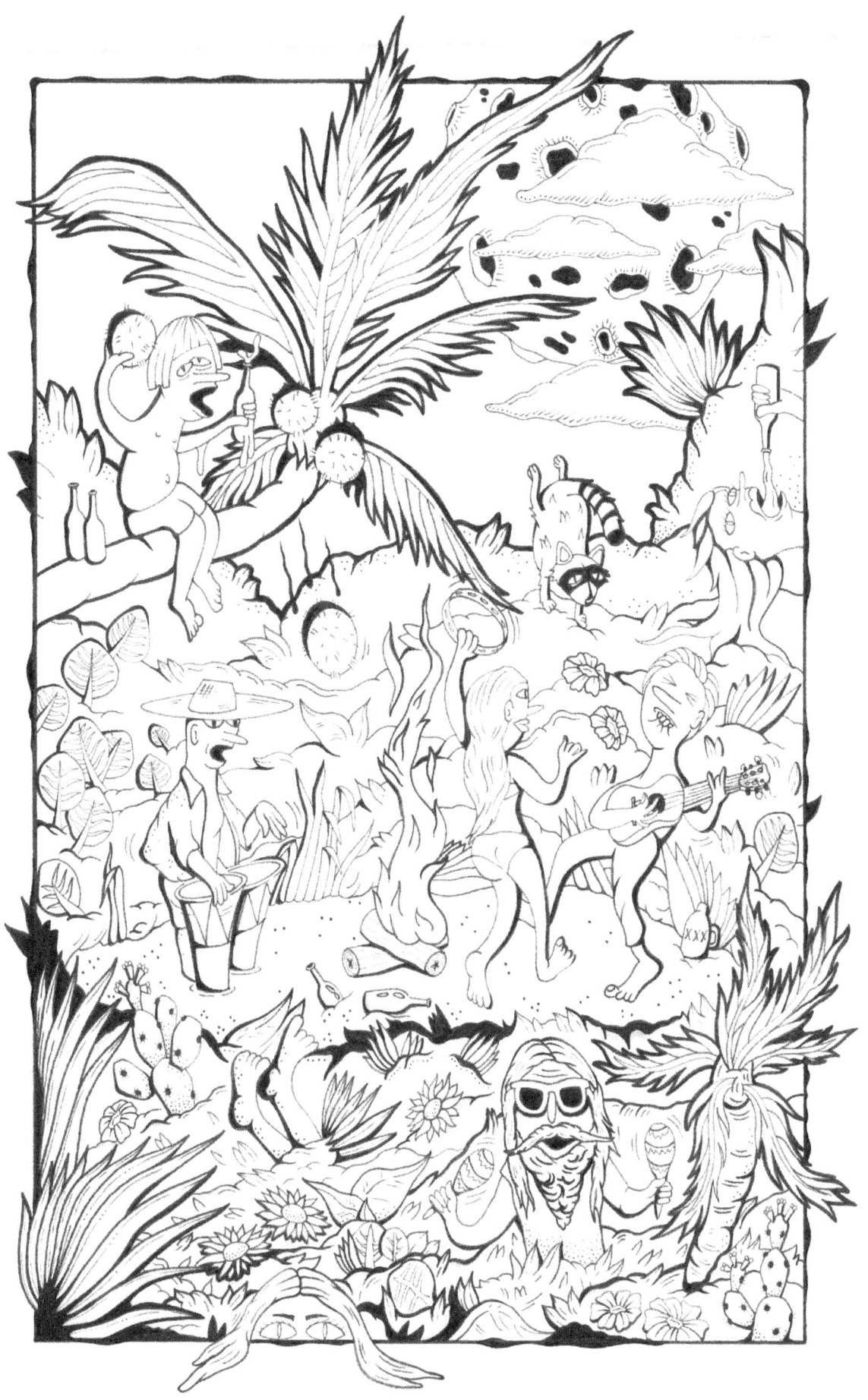

A fire lit night under the moon

Calls for a dip, the next day around noon

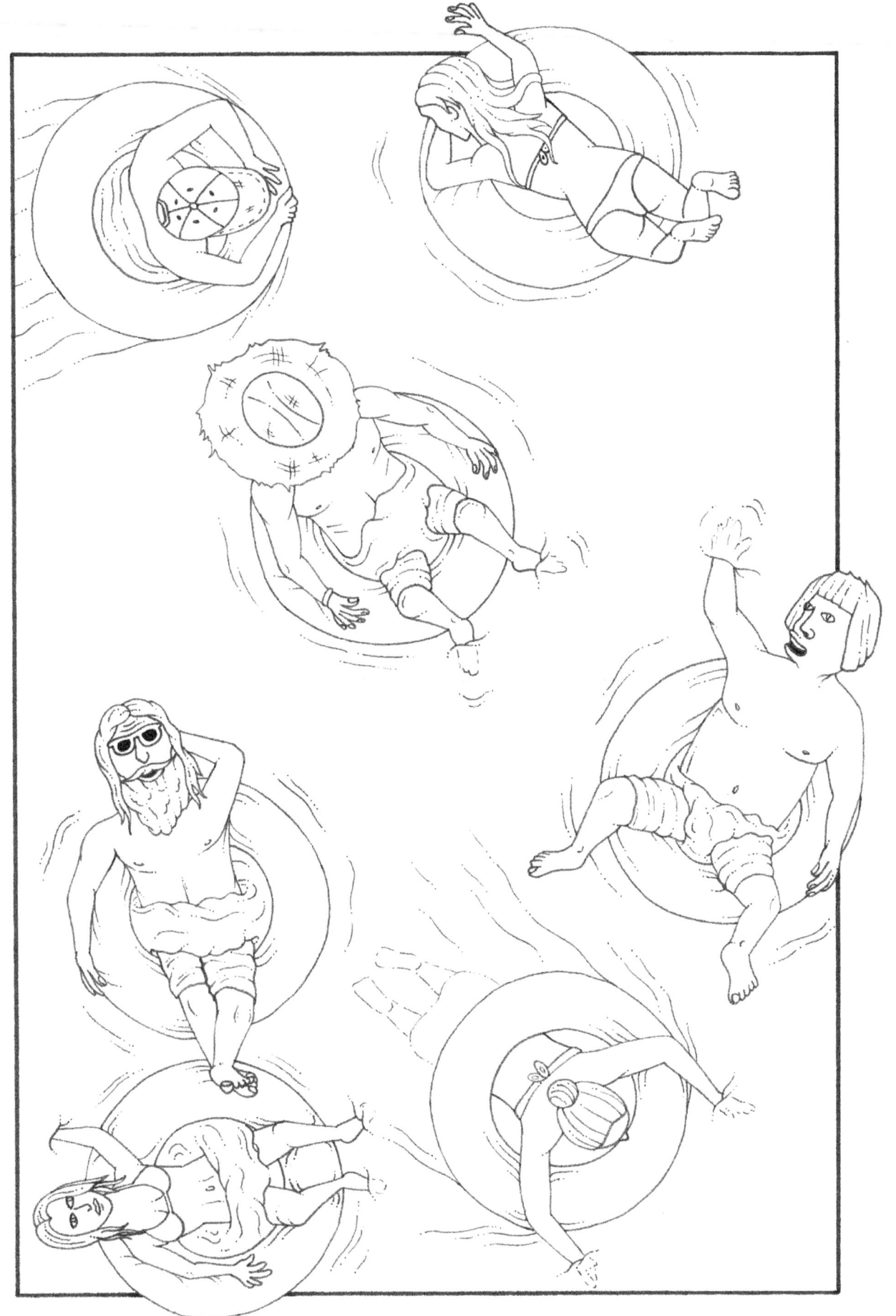

Tropical day-dreams...

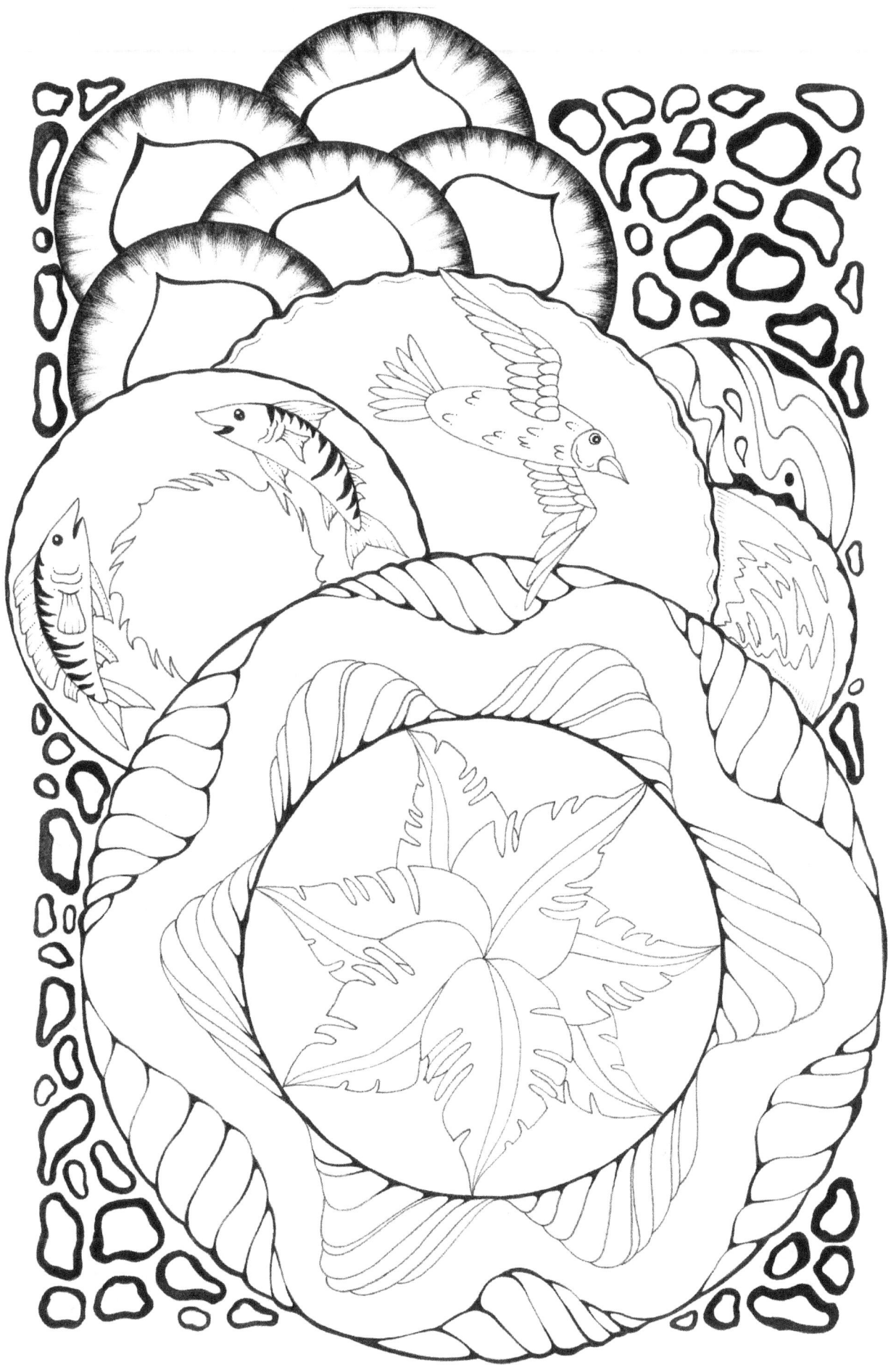

...and a hidden paradise

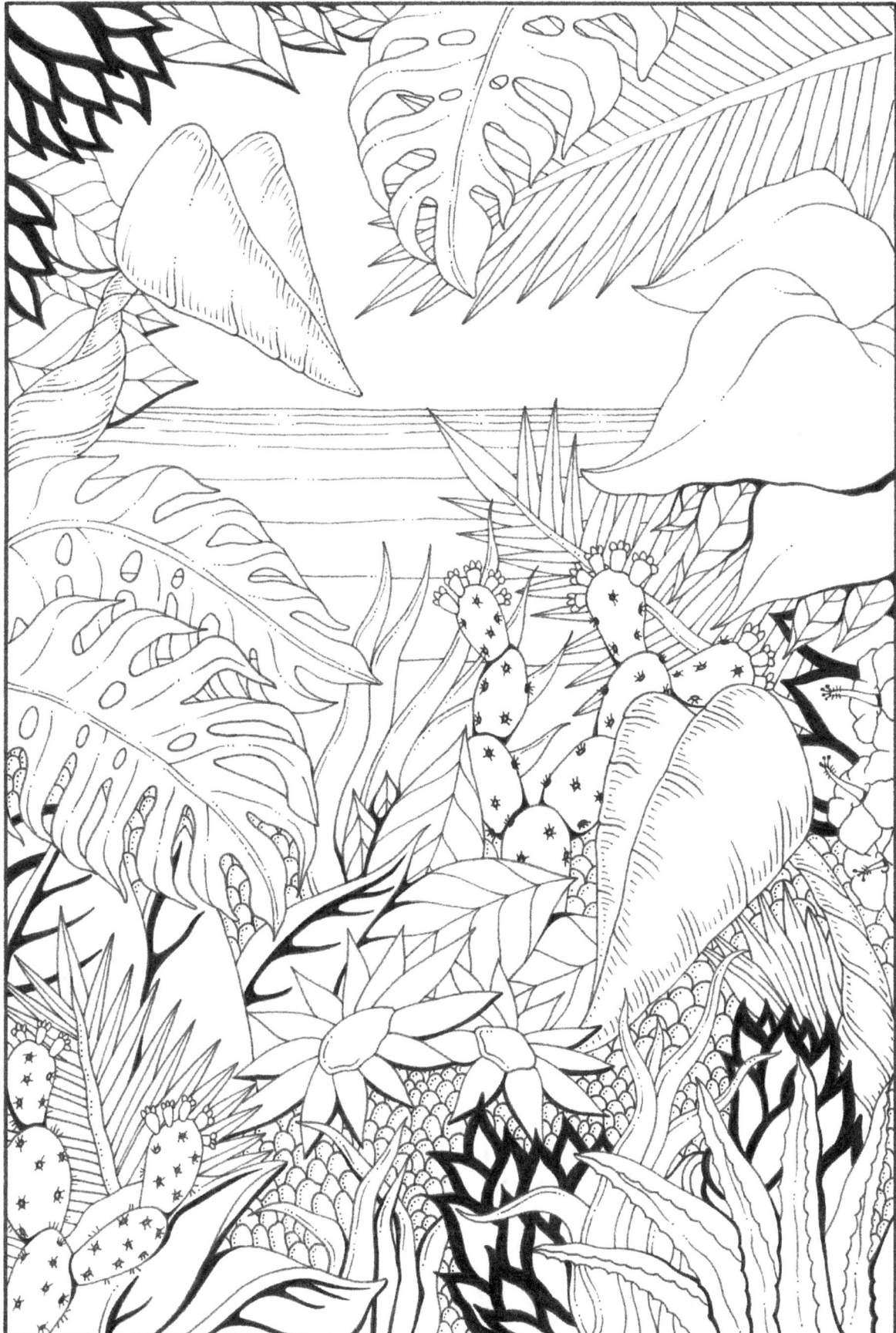

I've got the bungalow blues

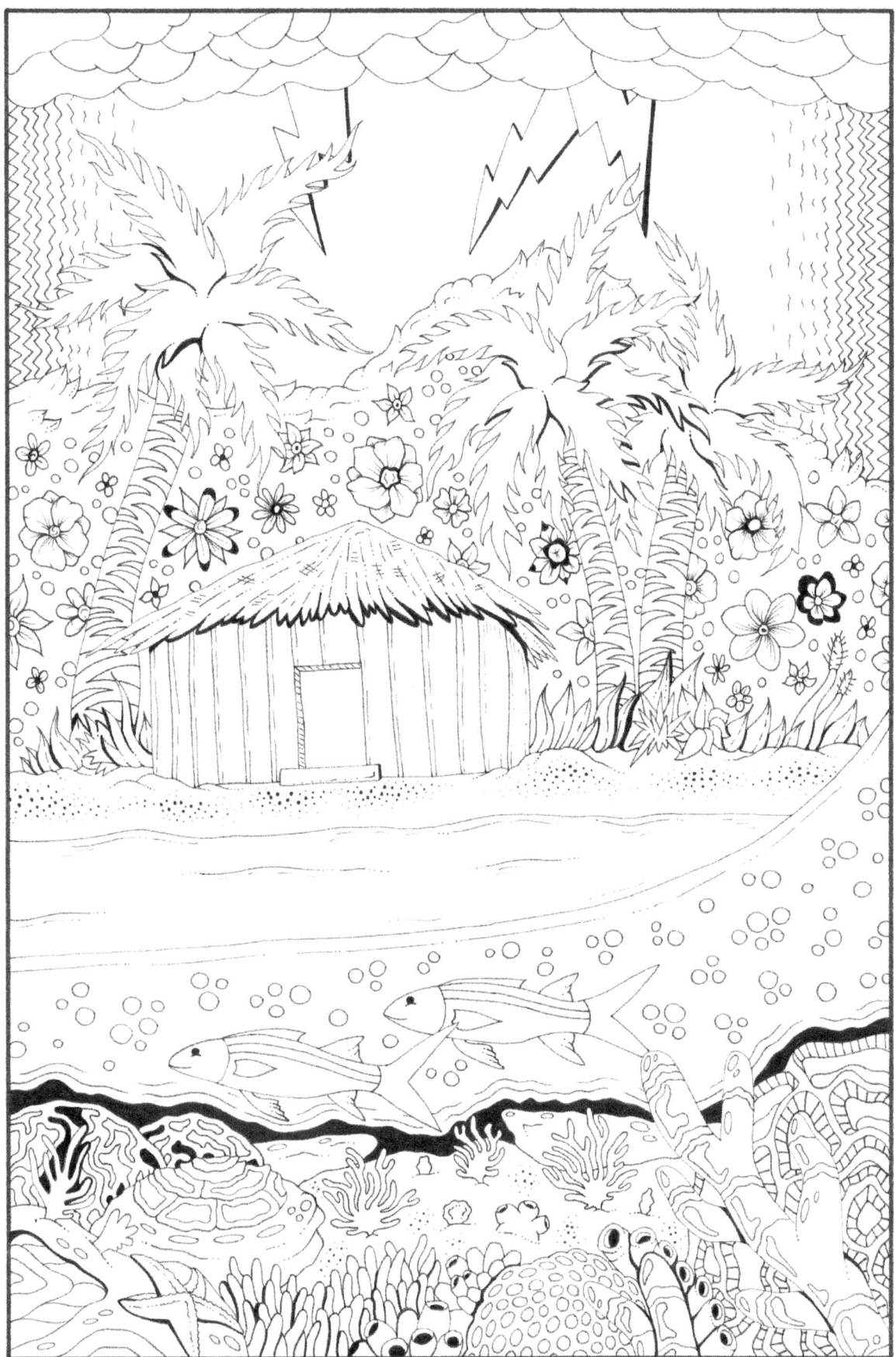

This here dolphin rider is Jen

She romps and plays with her dolphin friends

Looks like a lot of dol-fun eh?

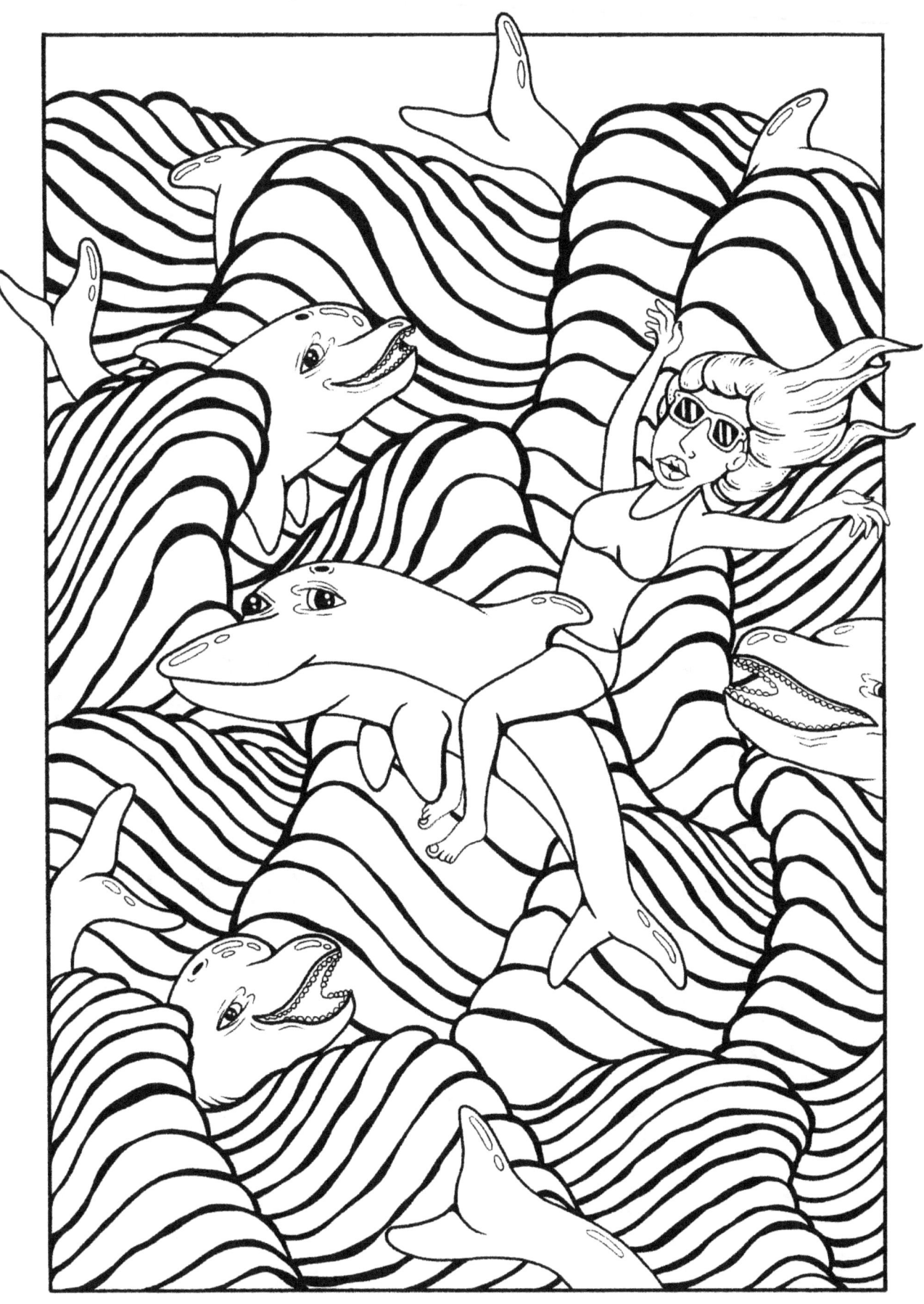

Collecting sea shells sure is swell

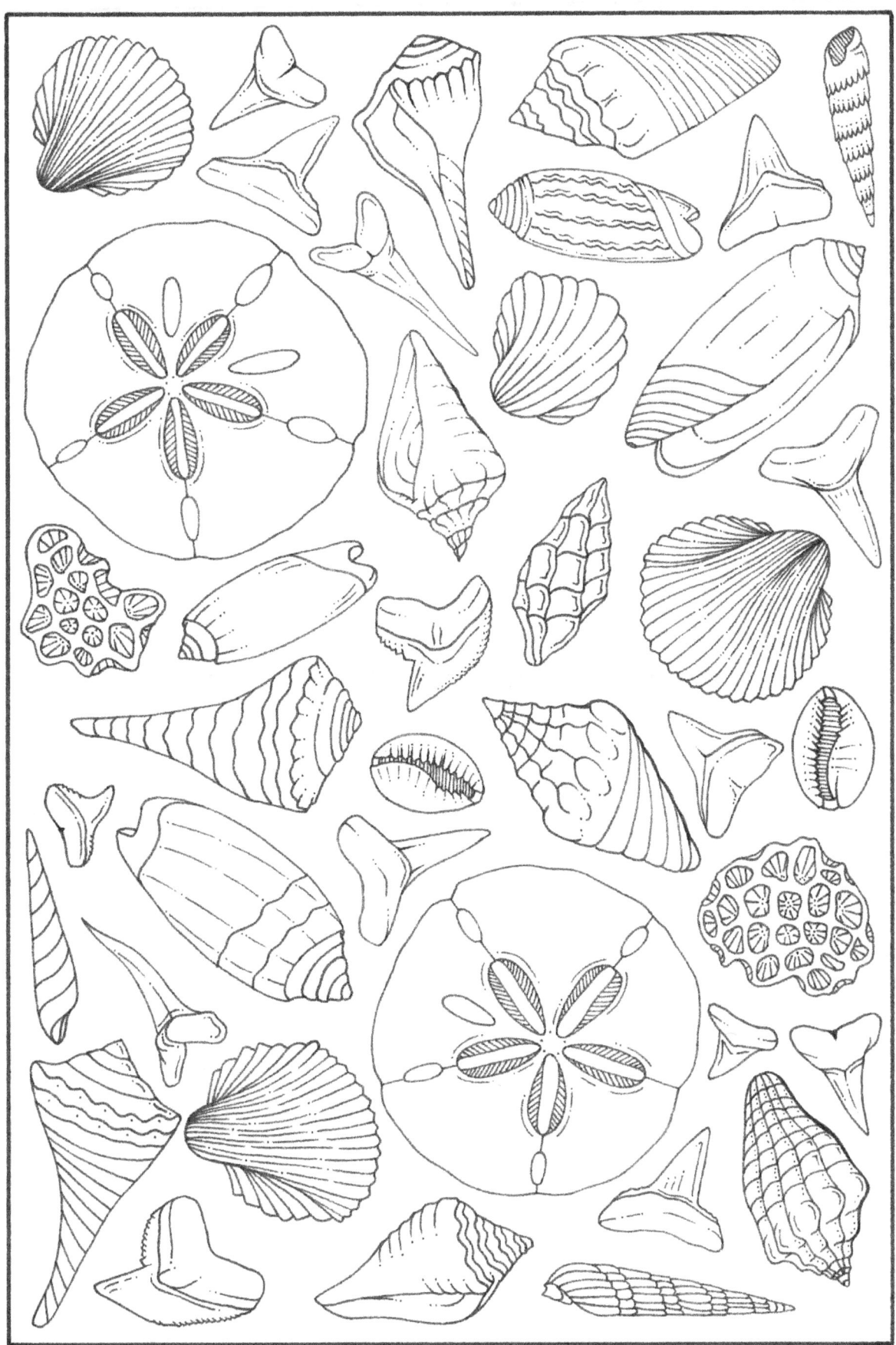

Just look at those pearly whites

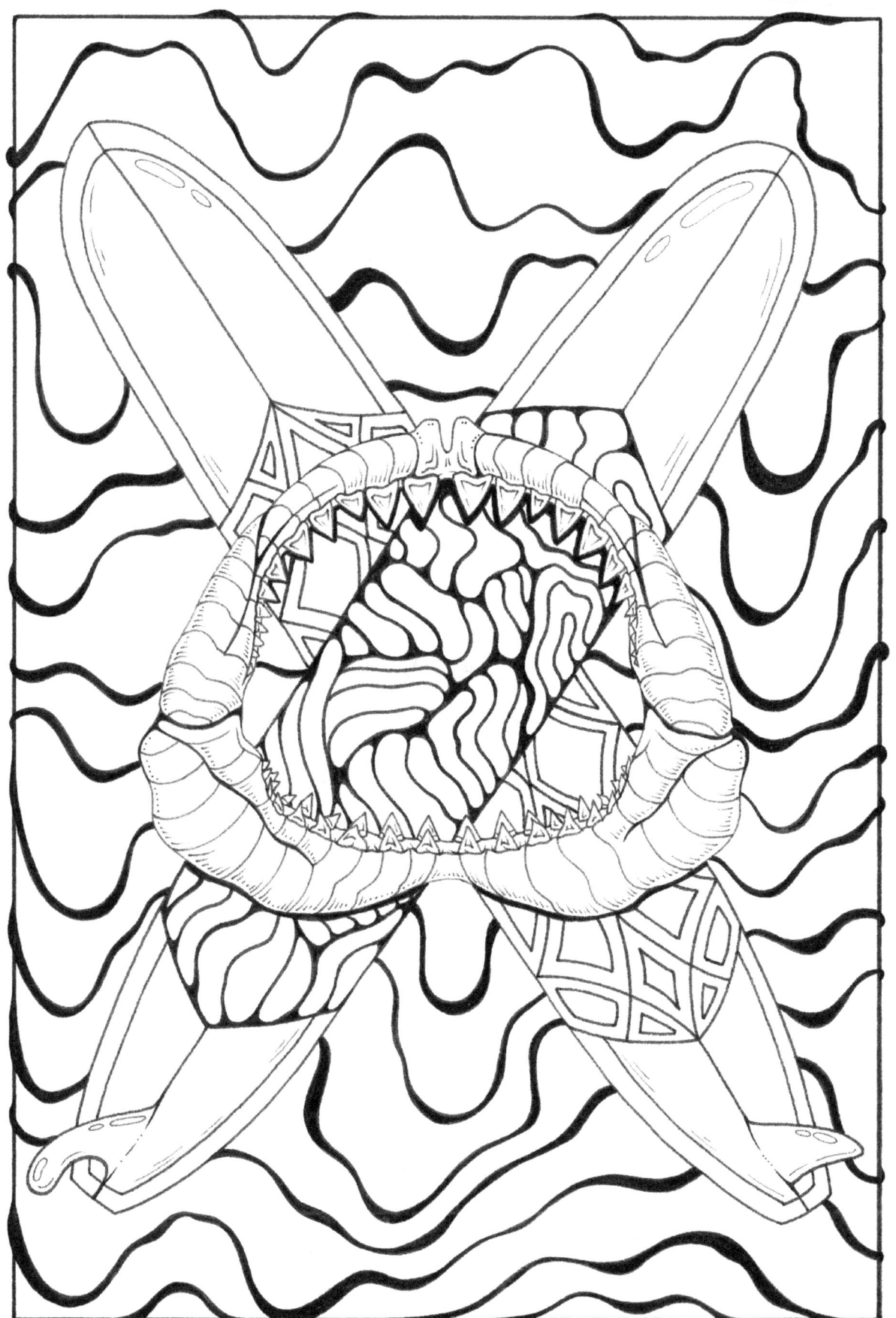

TIDAL WAVE!

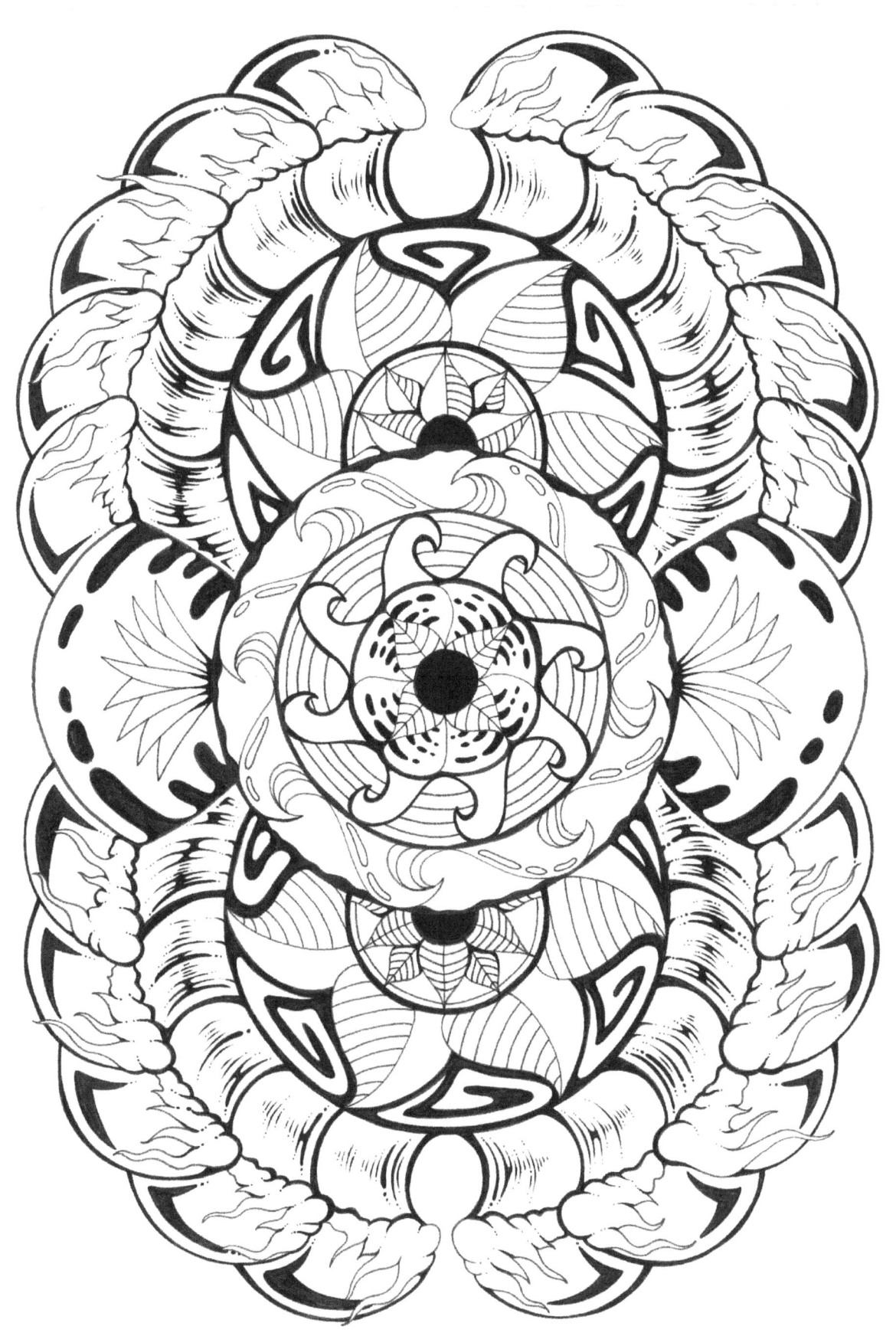

The endless summer daze

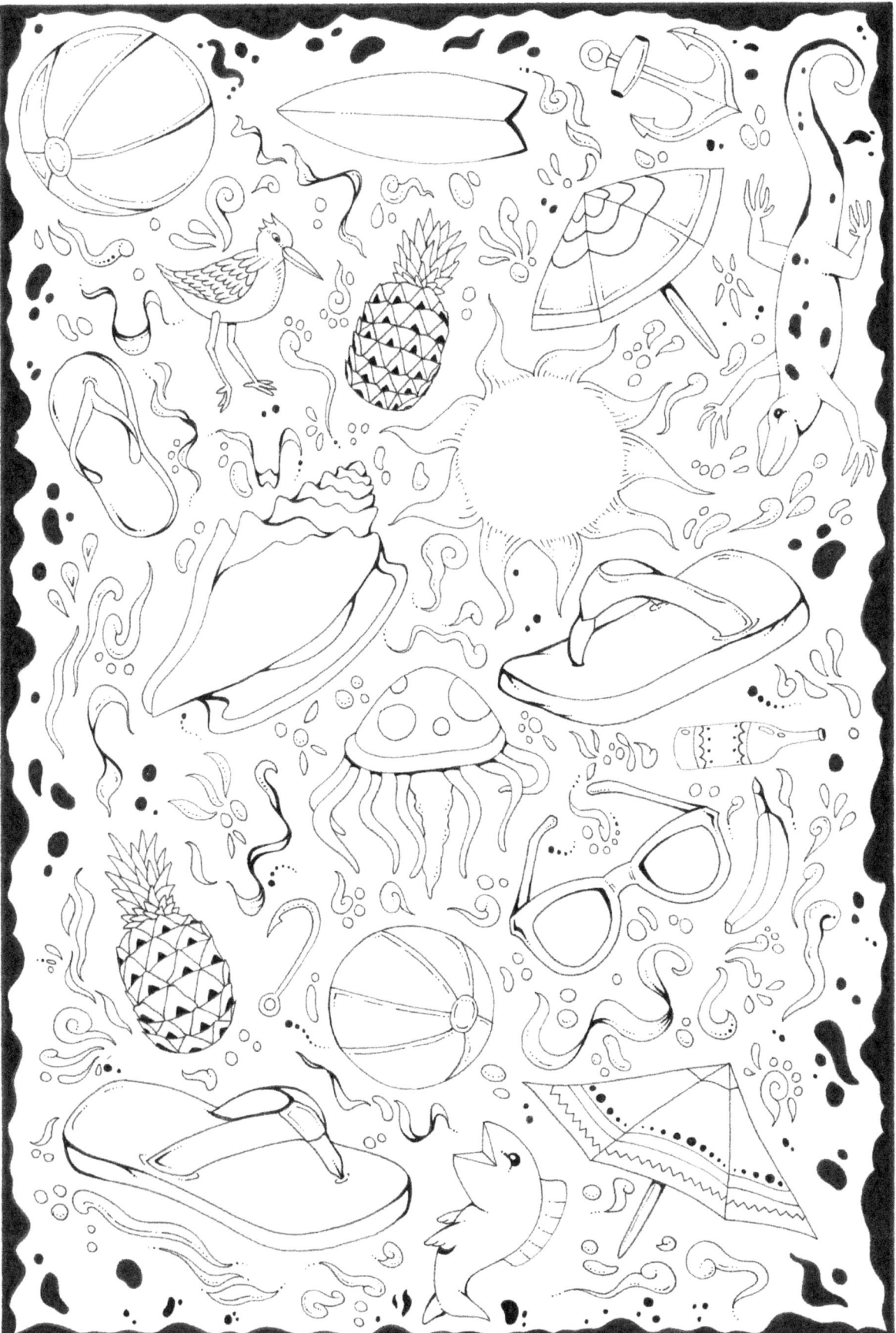

Scuba Steve went for a dive

Will Scuba Steve get out alive?

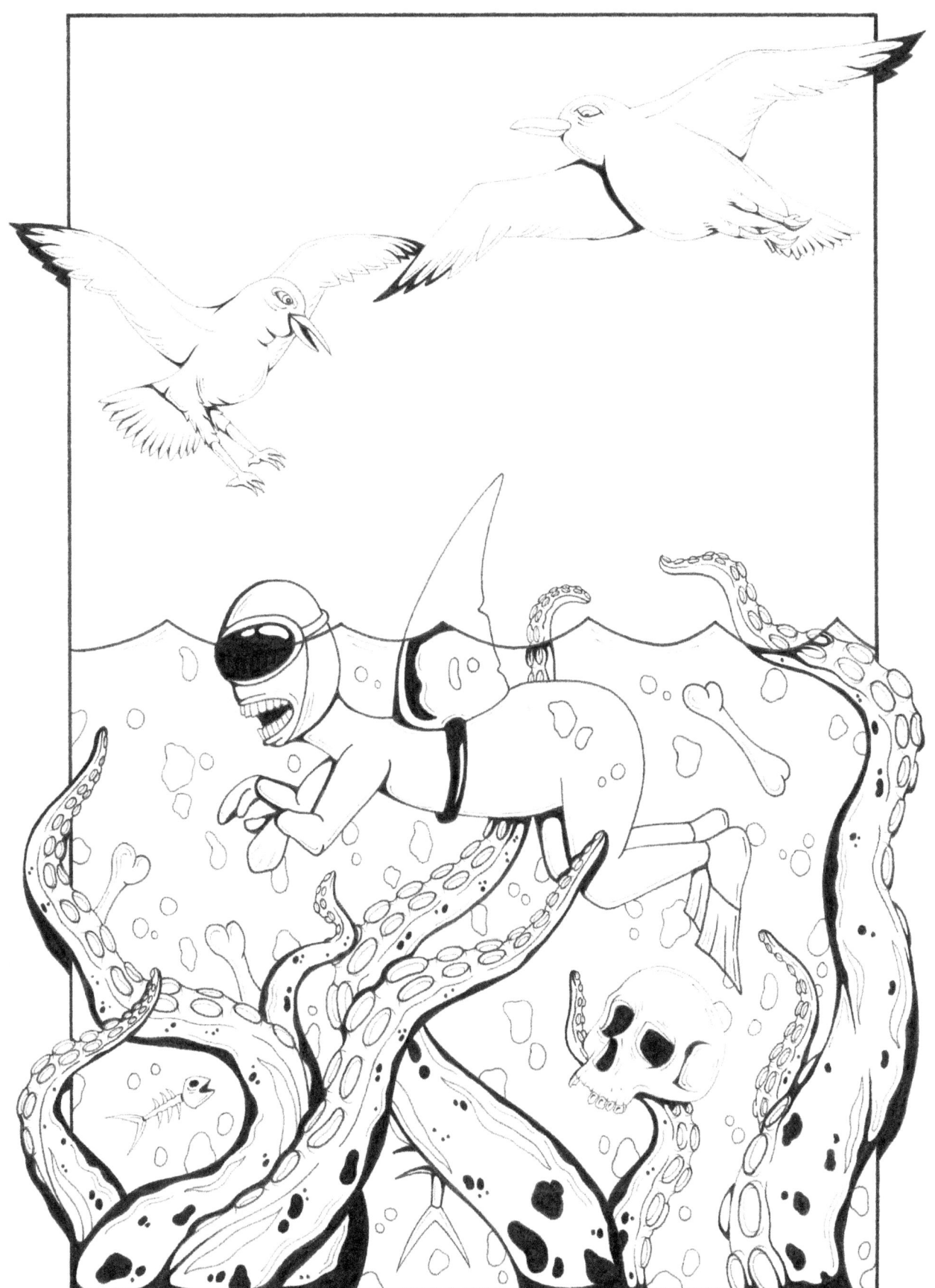

Kayakin' Kenny paddled into the cove

Those pesky sharks are coming in droves!

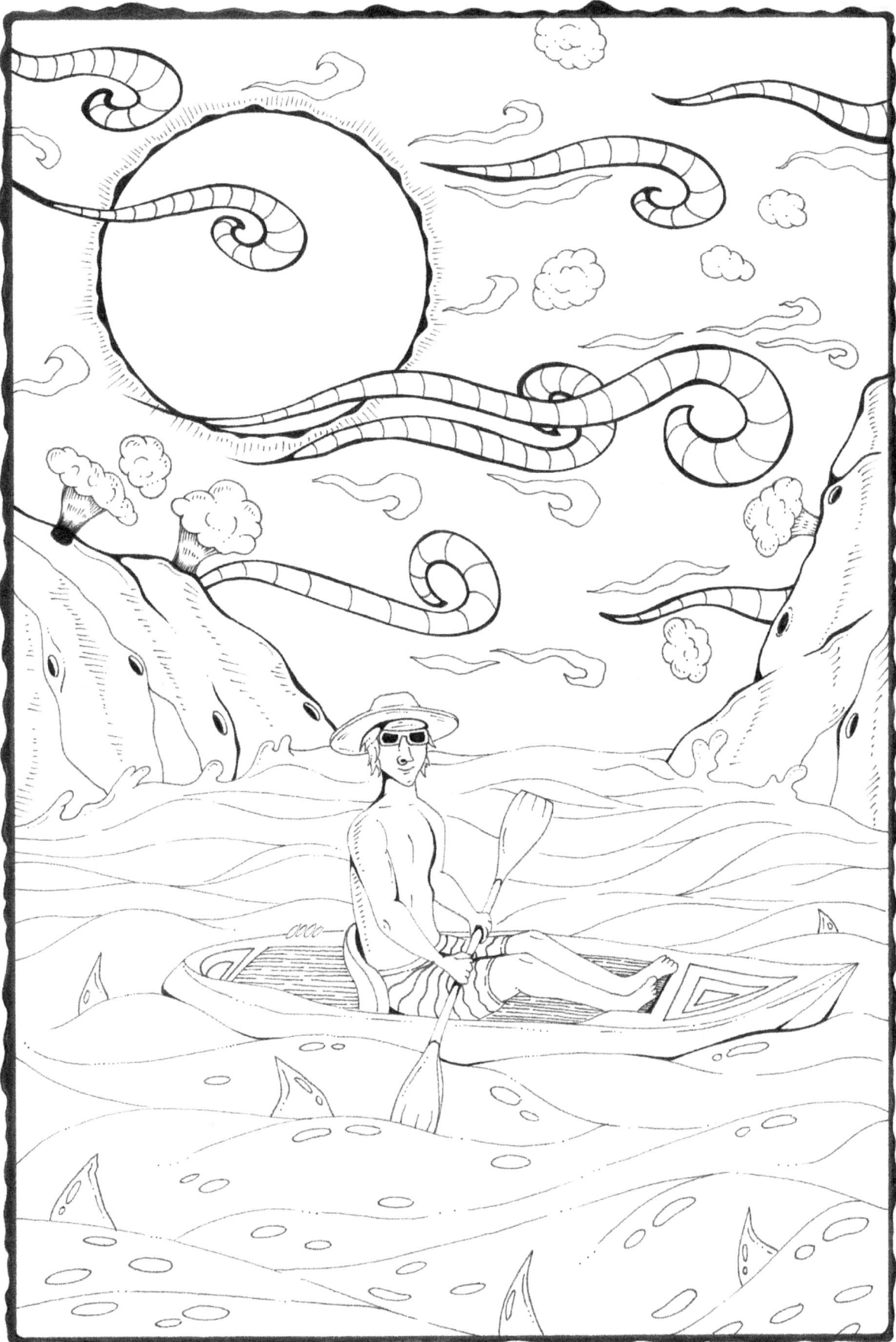

There are some crazy crustaceans creeping around

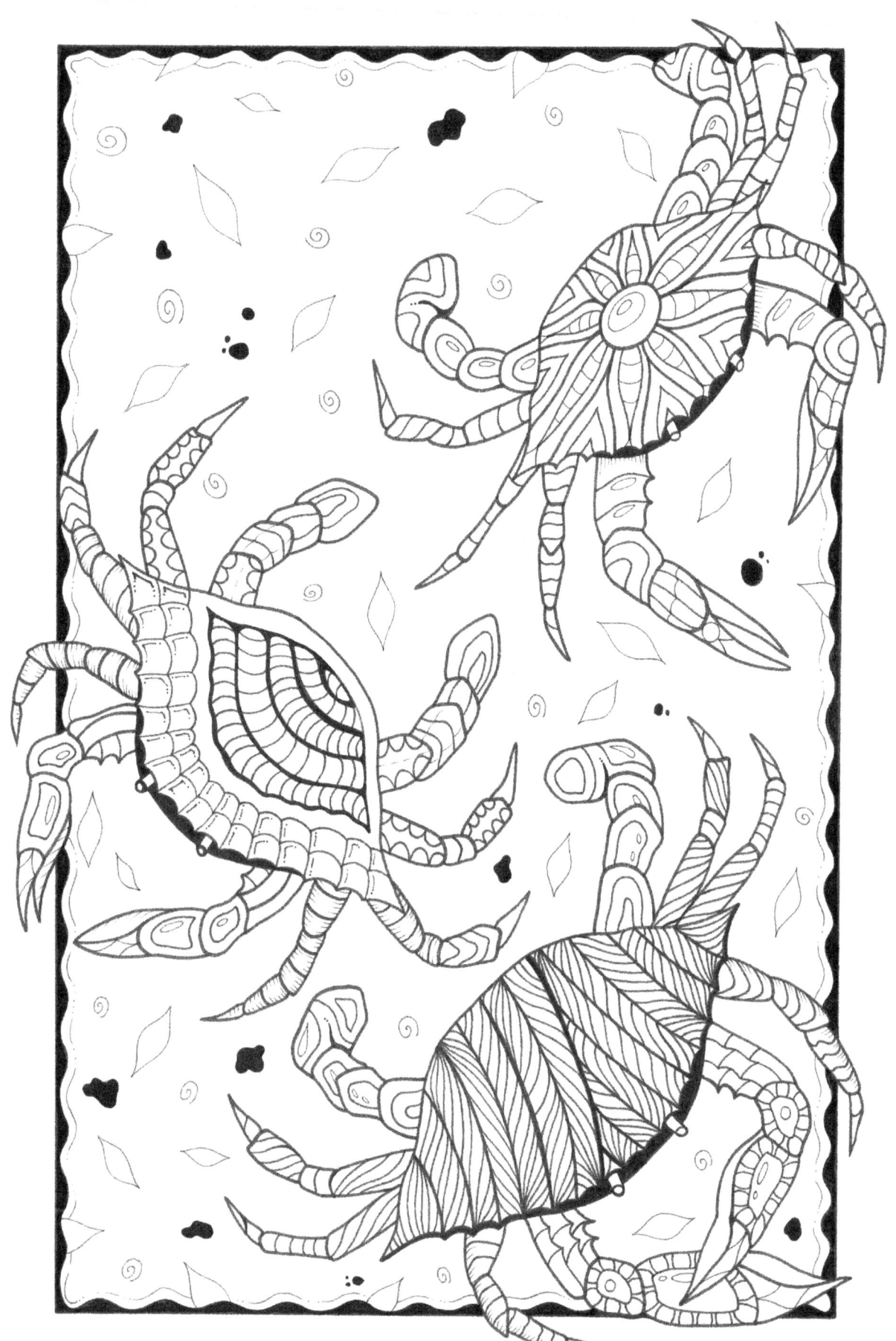

Time for a board meeting

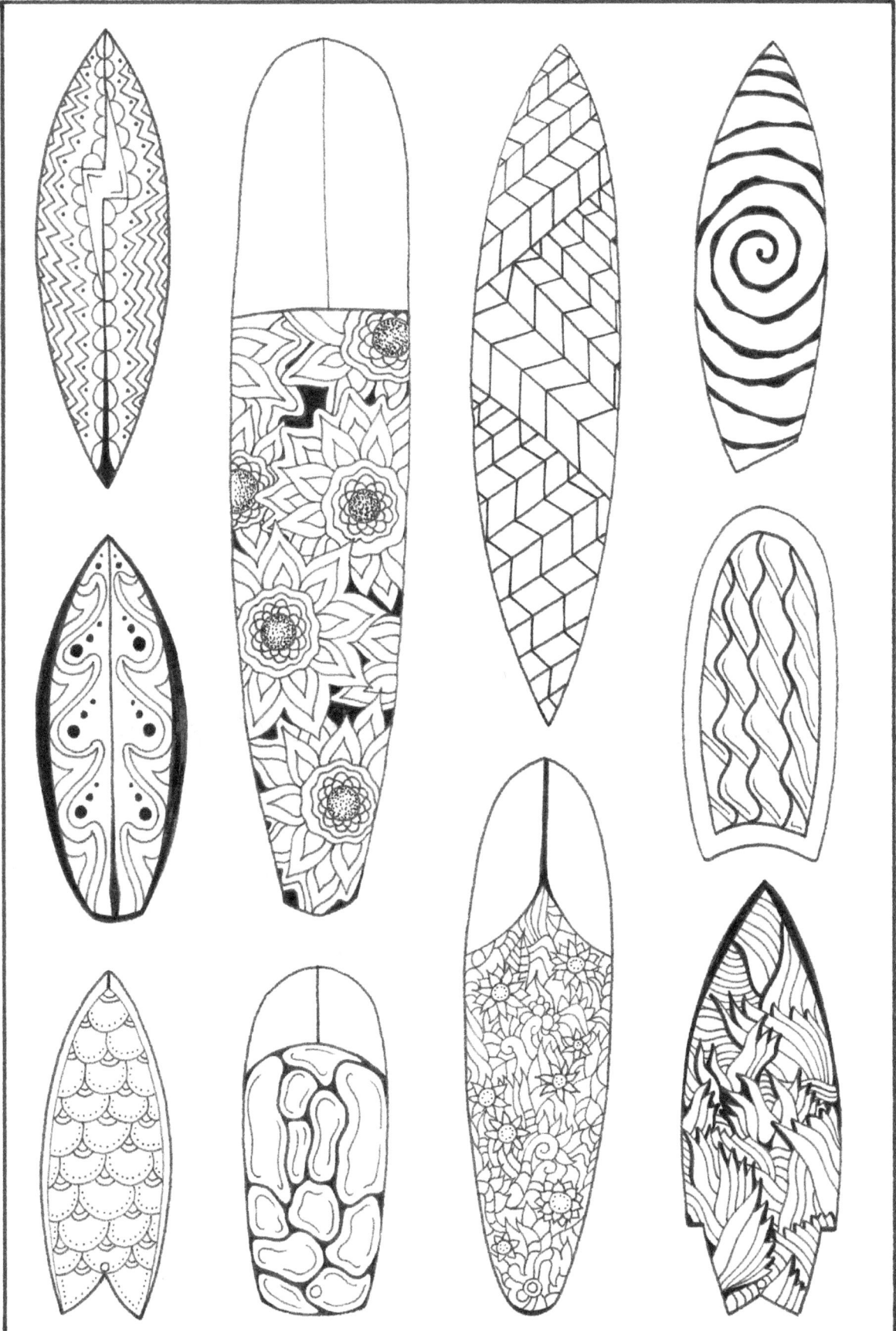

There's no doubt in our minds that he's the king of the sea

King Neptune will shred and make it look easy

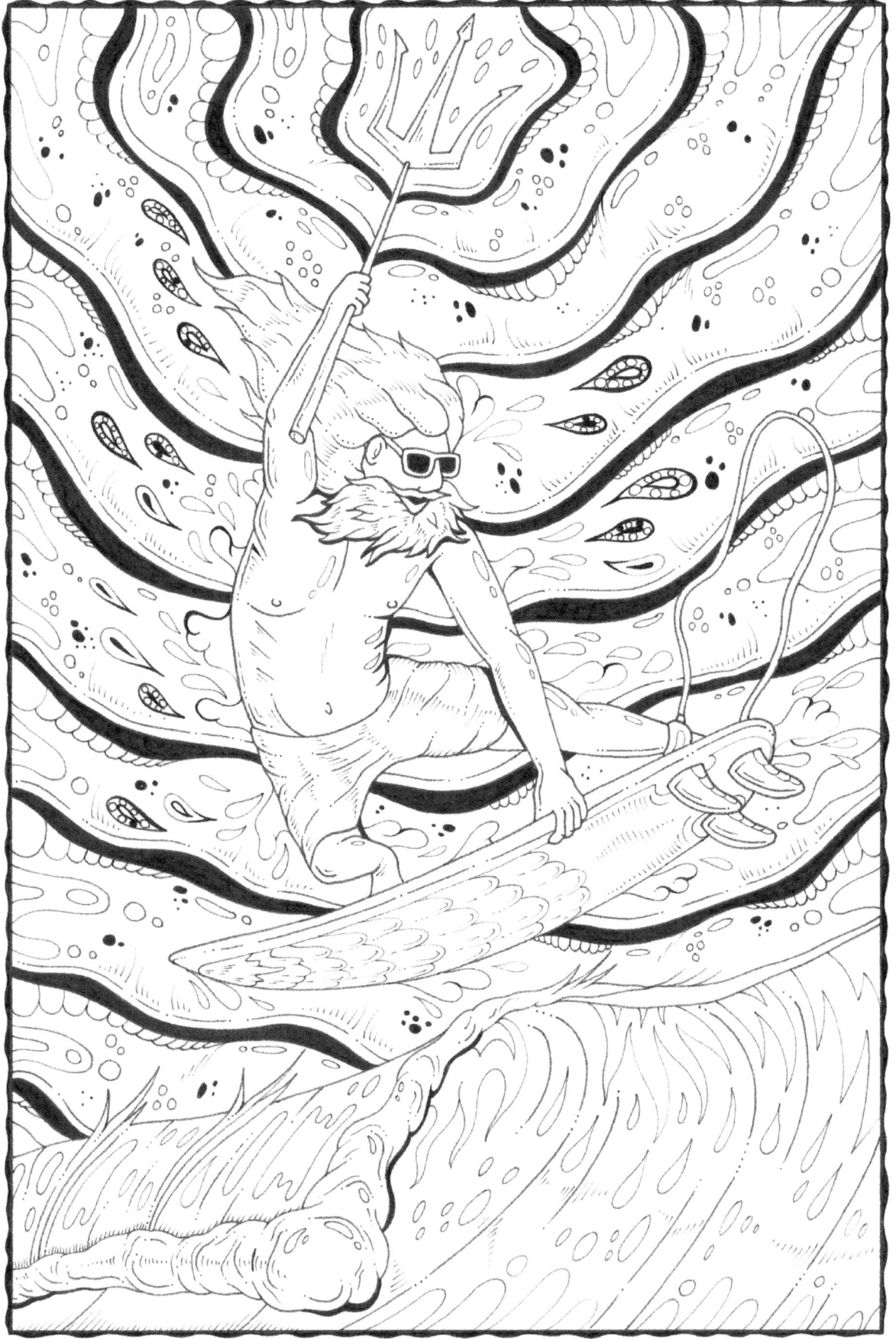

A day with the fishes is all that me wishes

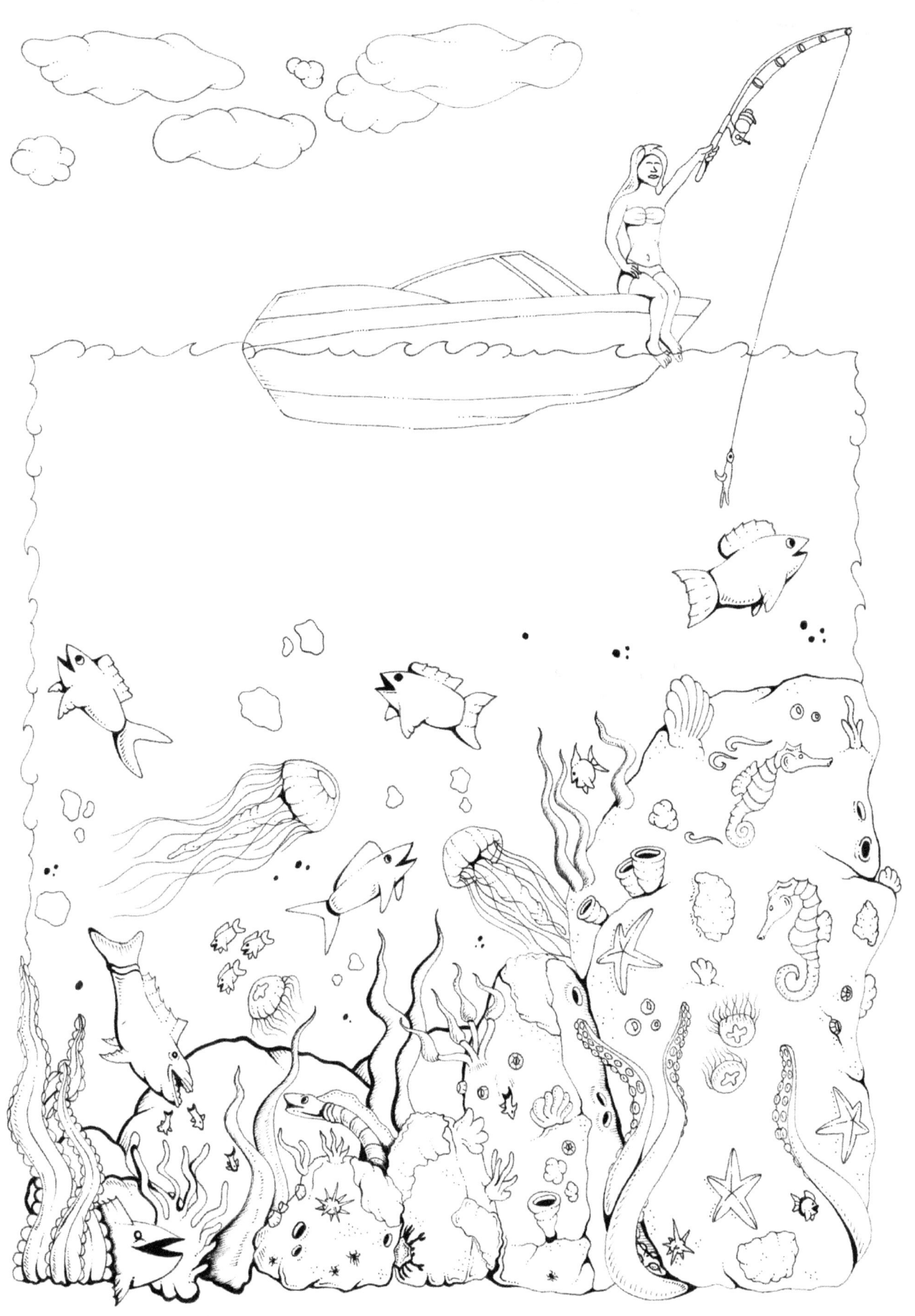

Would you like some jelly with that?

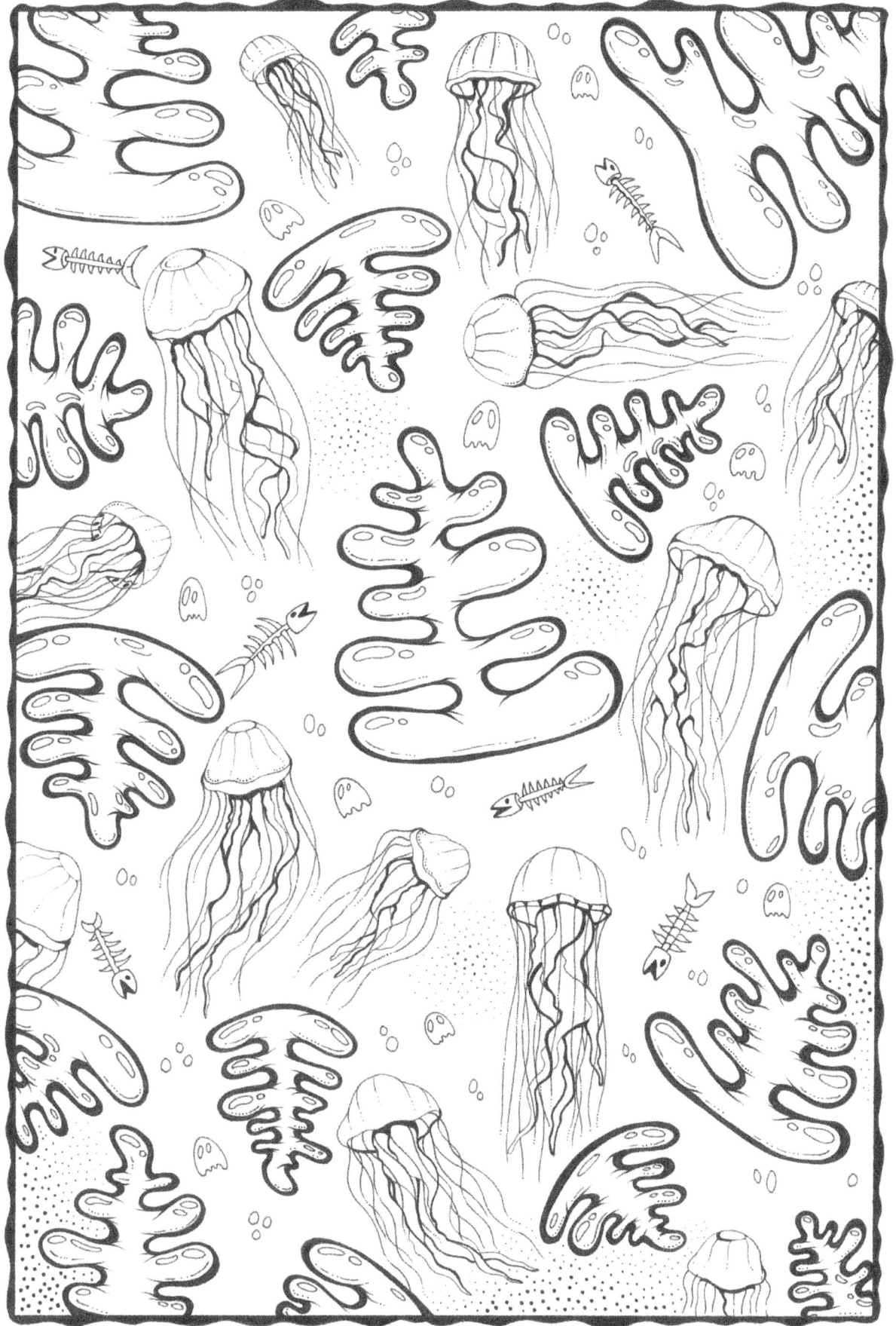

pelican pete moves his feet to the beat

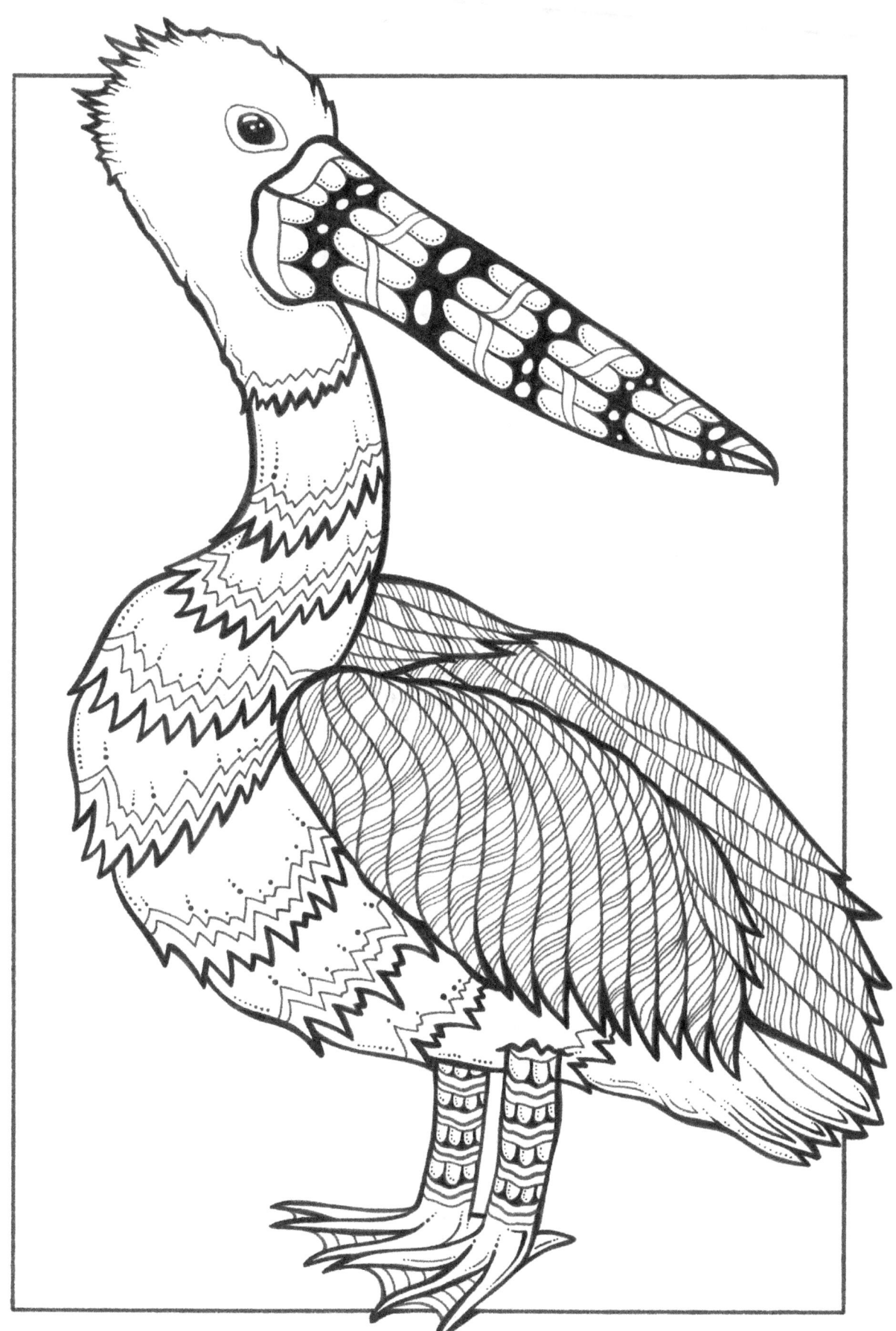

There's something fishy going on here...

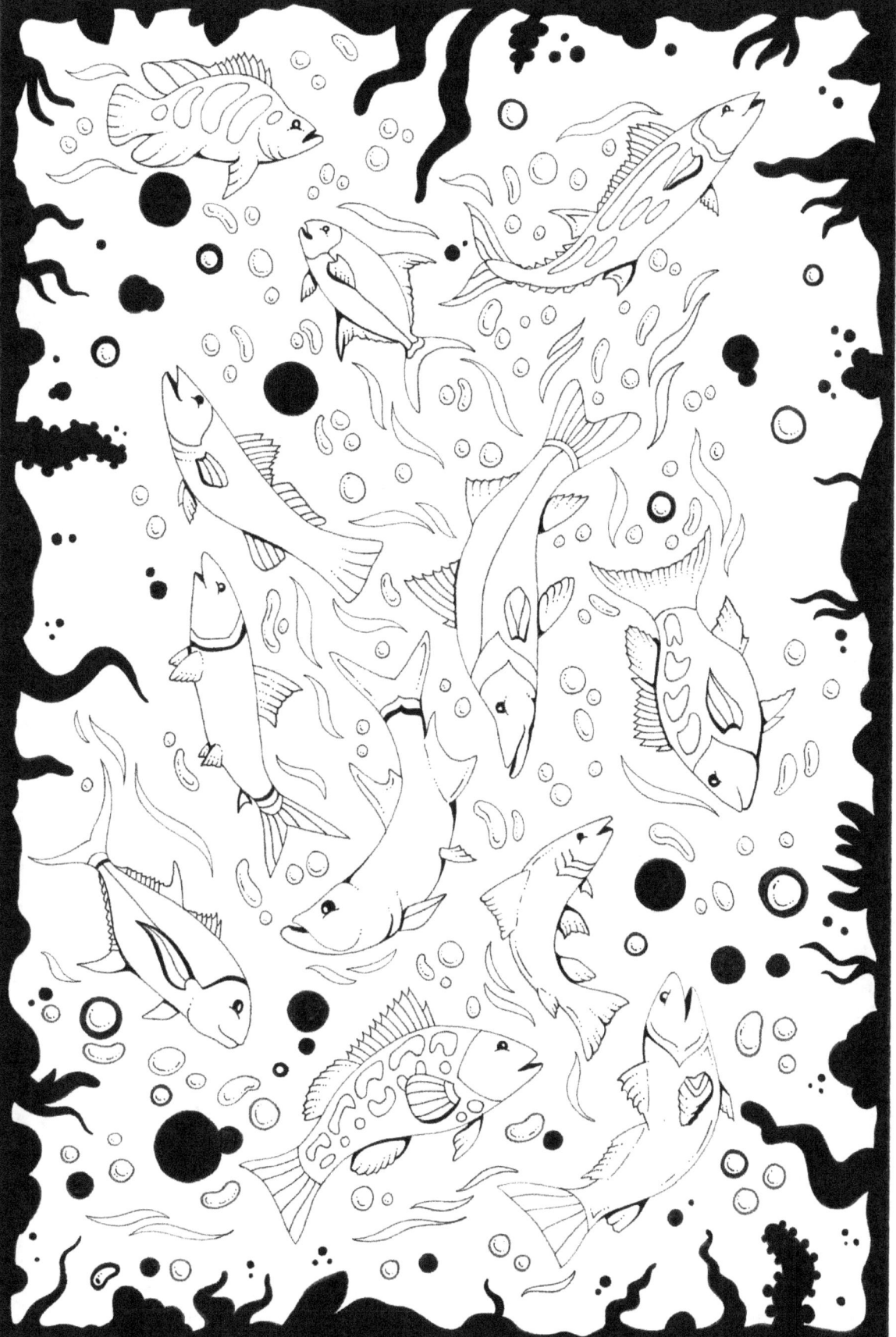

...and quit your monkeyin' around!

You're driving me bananas

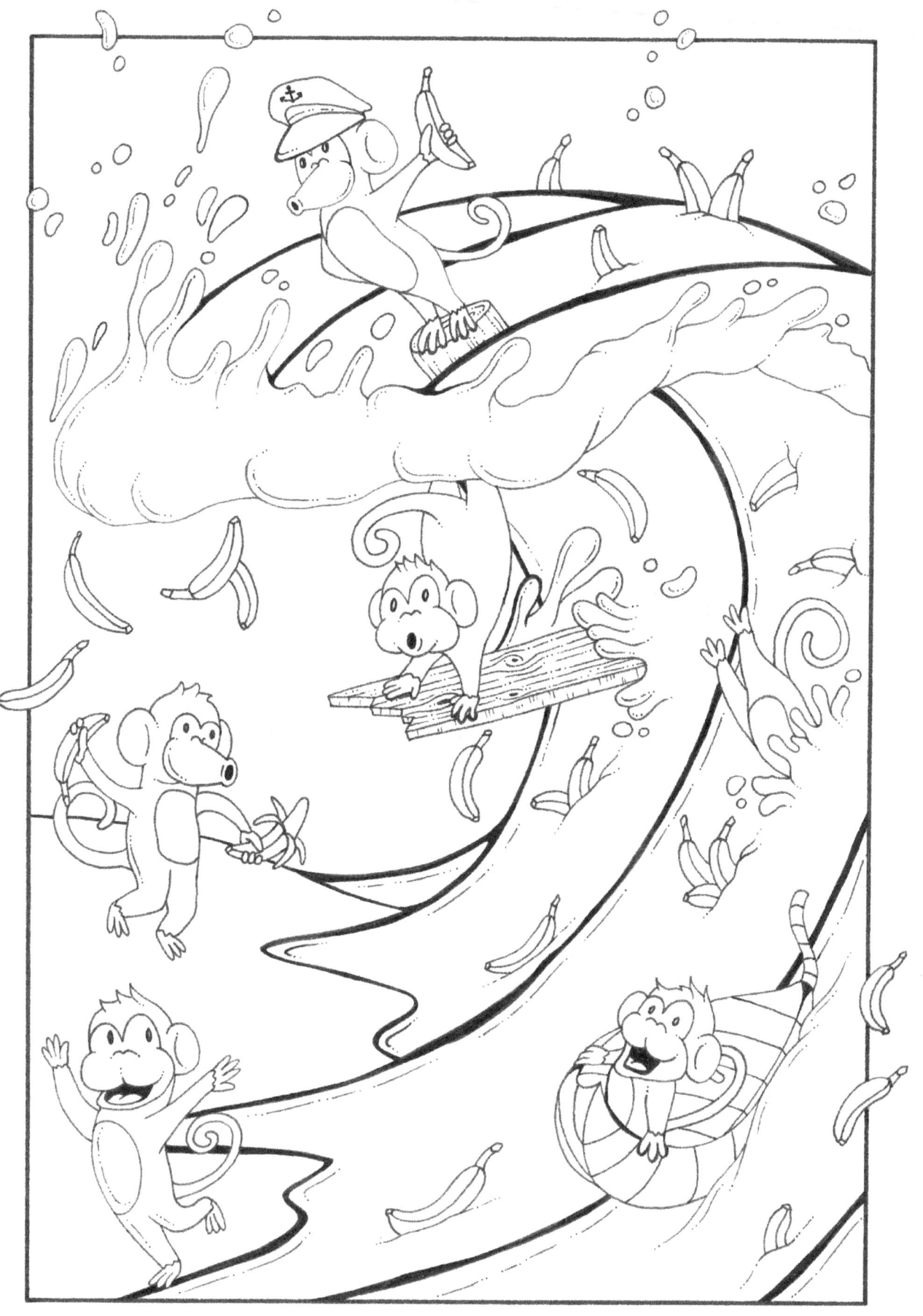

Sailing the seven seas is the ultimate test

So hoist your sails and head due west

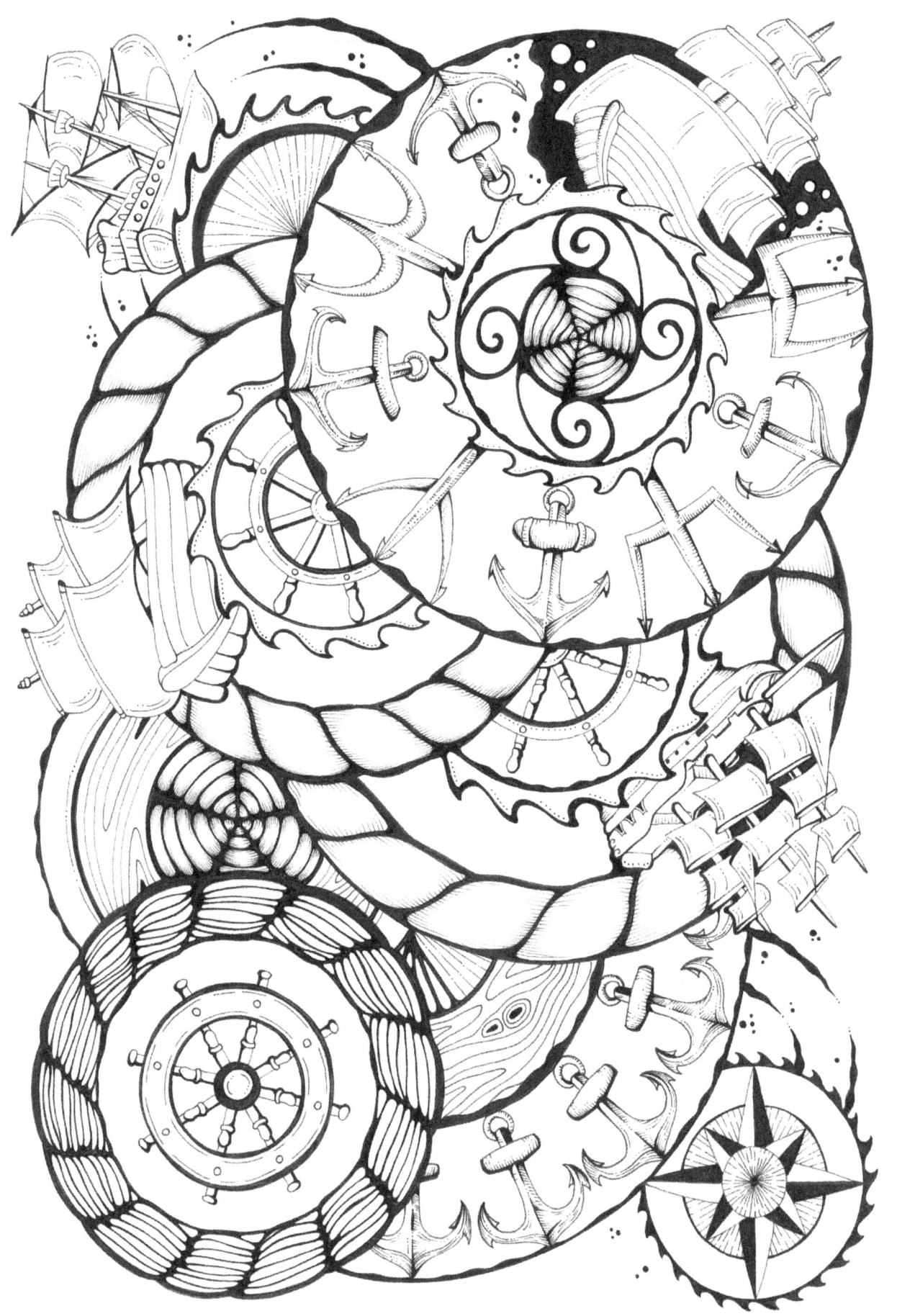

Now where did this fella wander off to?

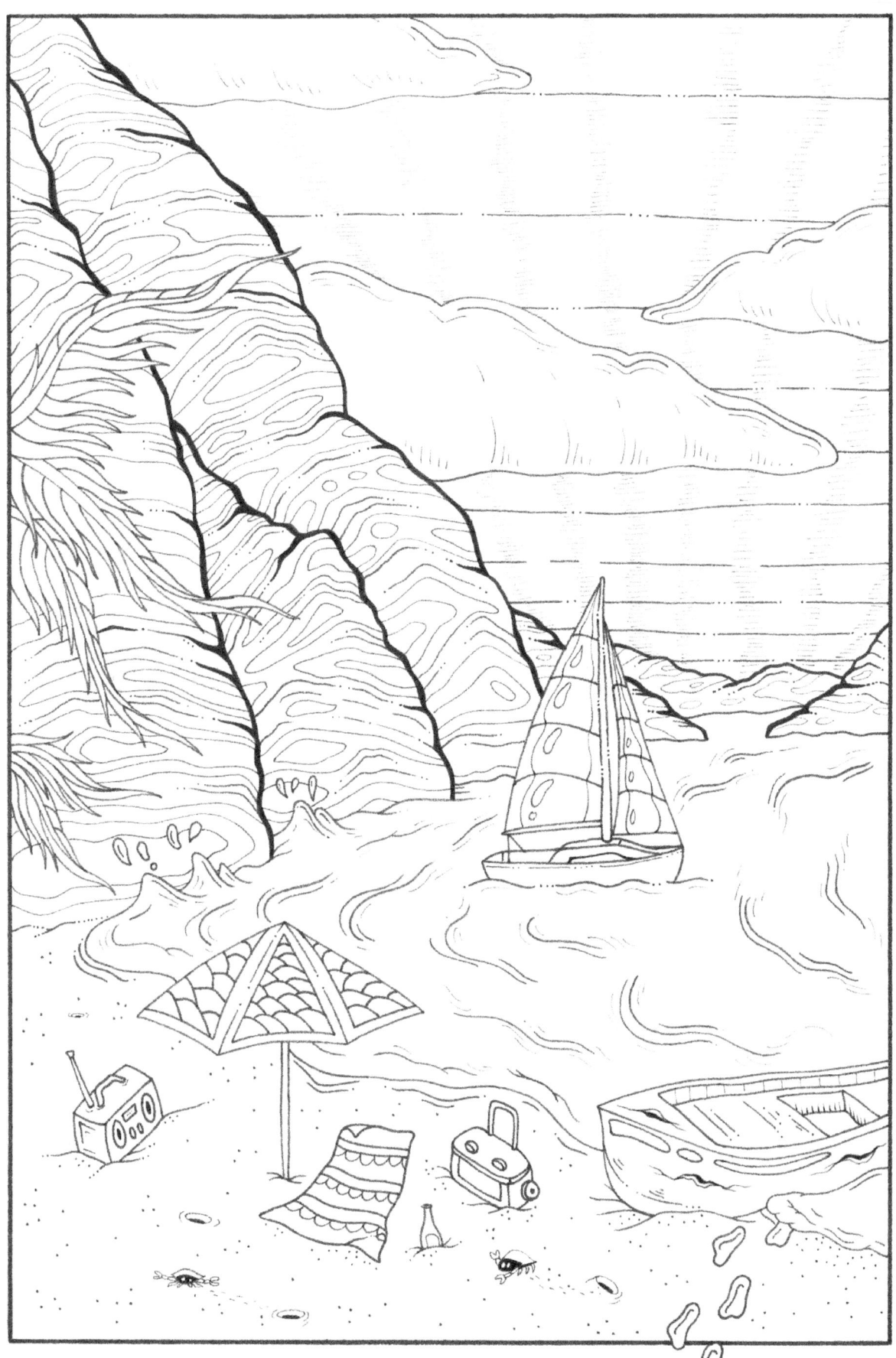

Relax and unwind amongst the sands of time

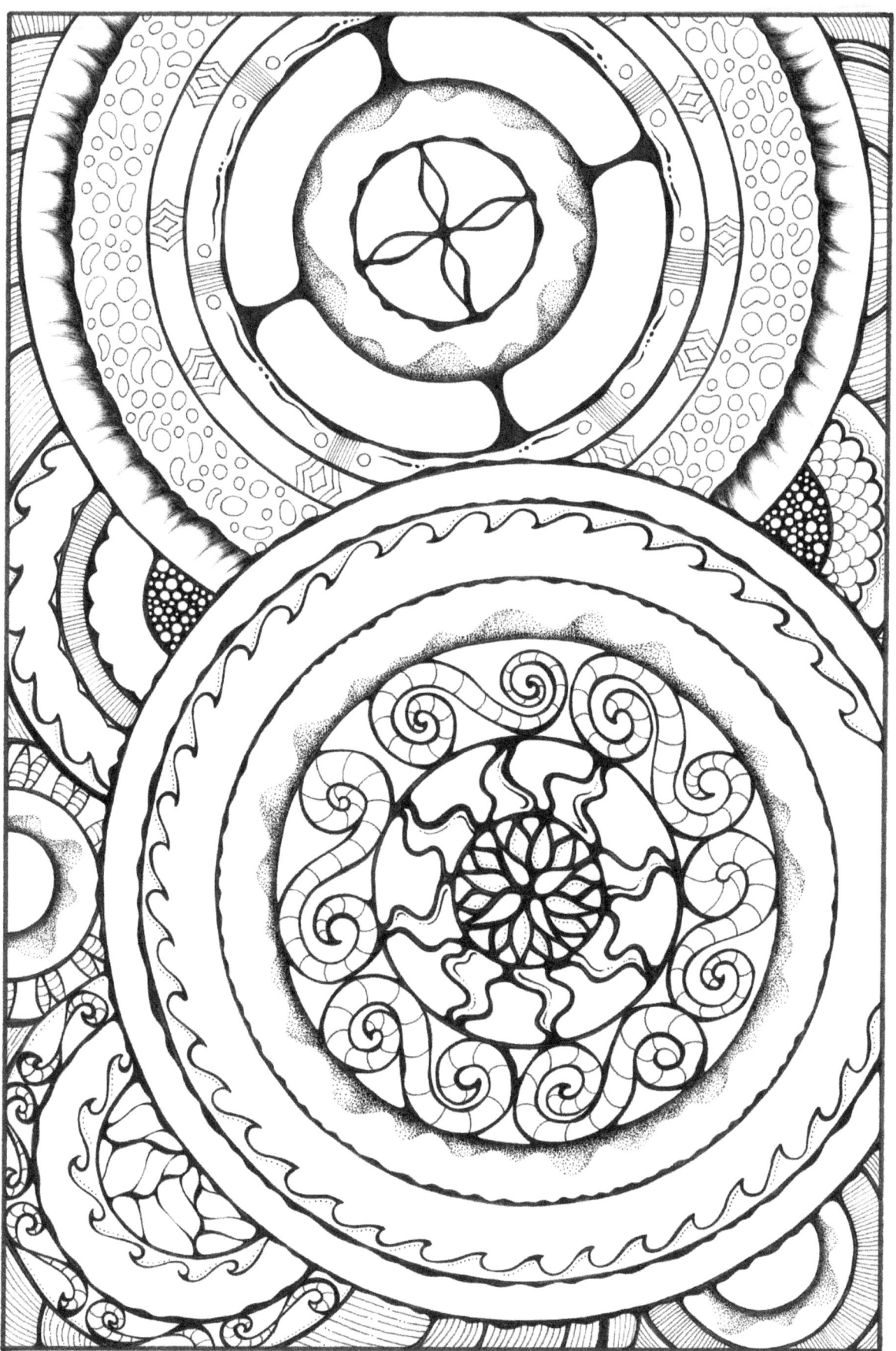

Ahhh, goo lagoon...

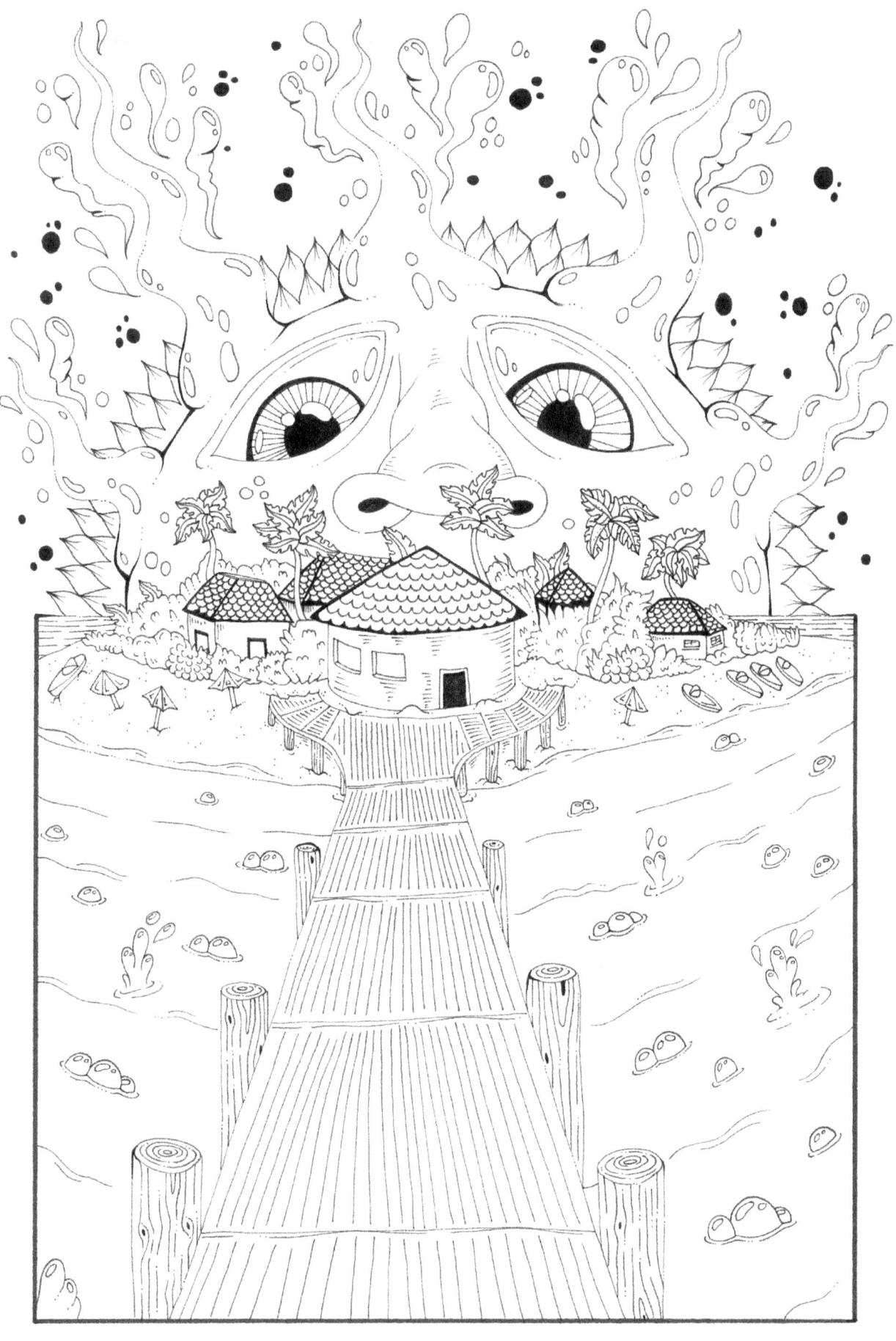

The best way to spend some time in the sand

Is to soak up some rays, with a drink in your hand

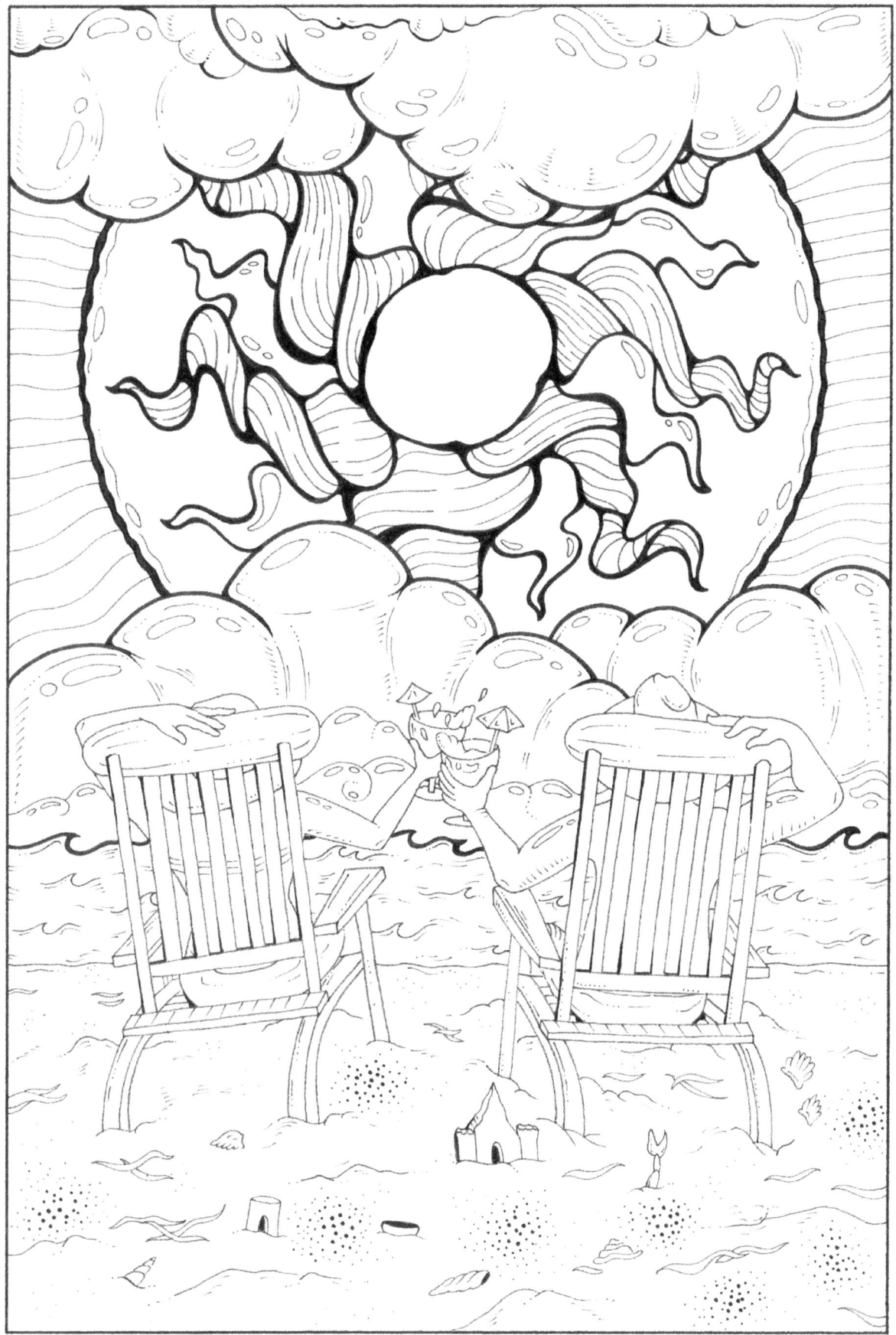

Don't stare at the sun

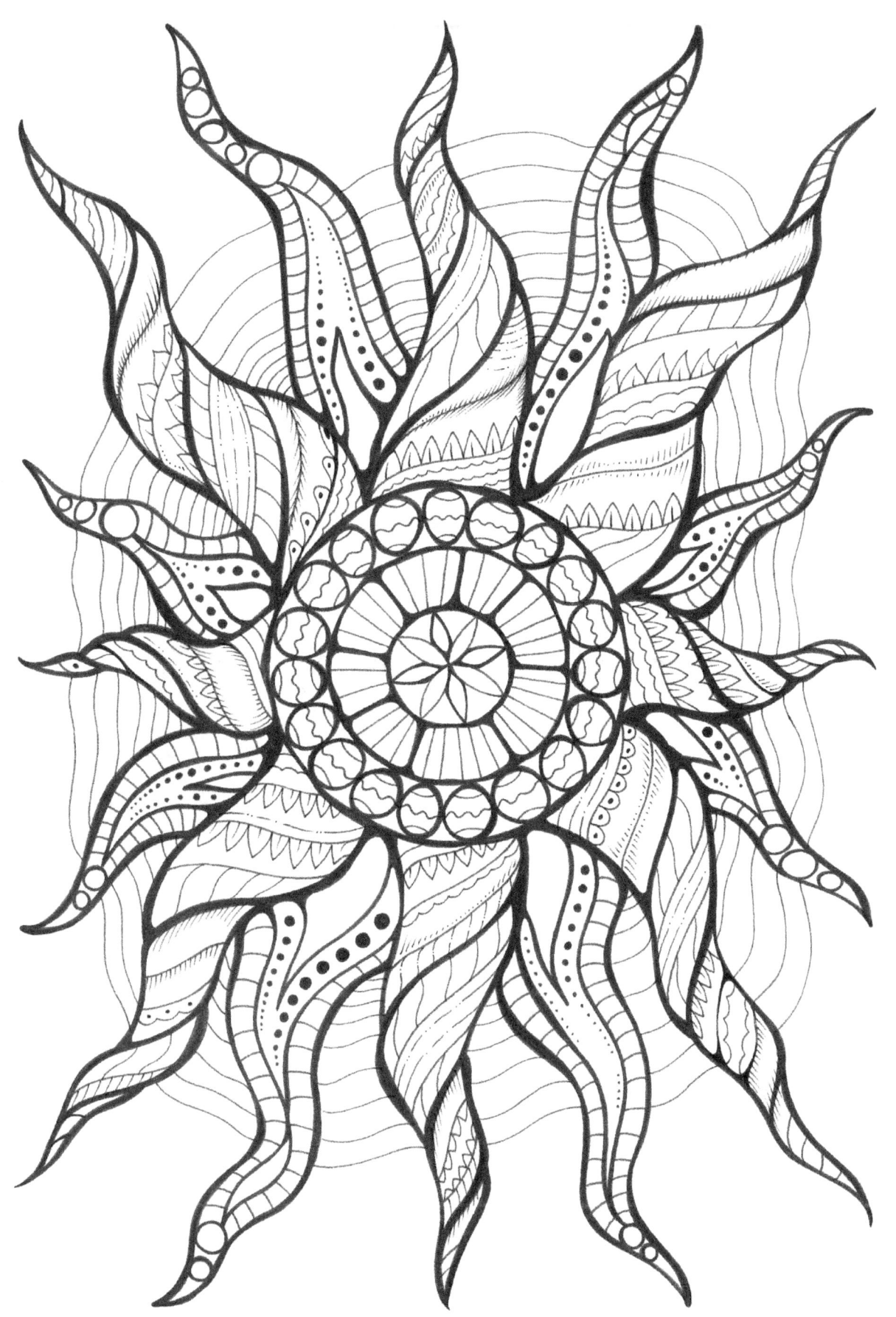

Sunset swells as far as the eye can SEA

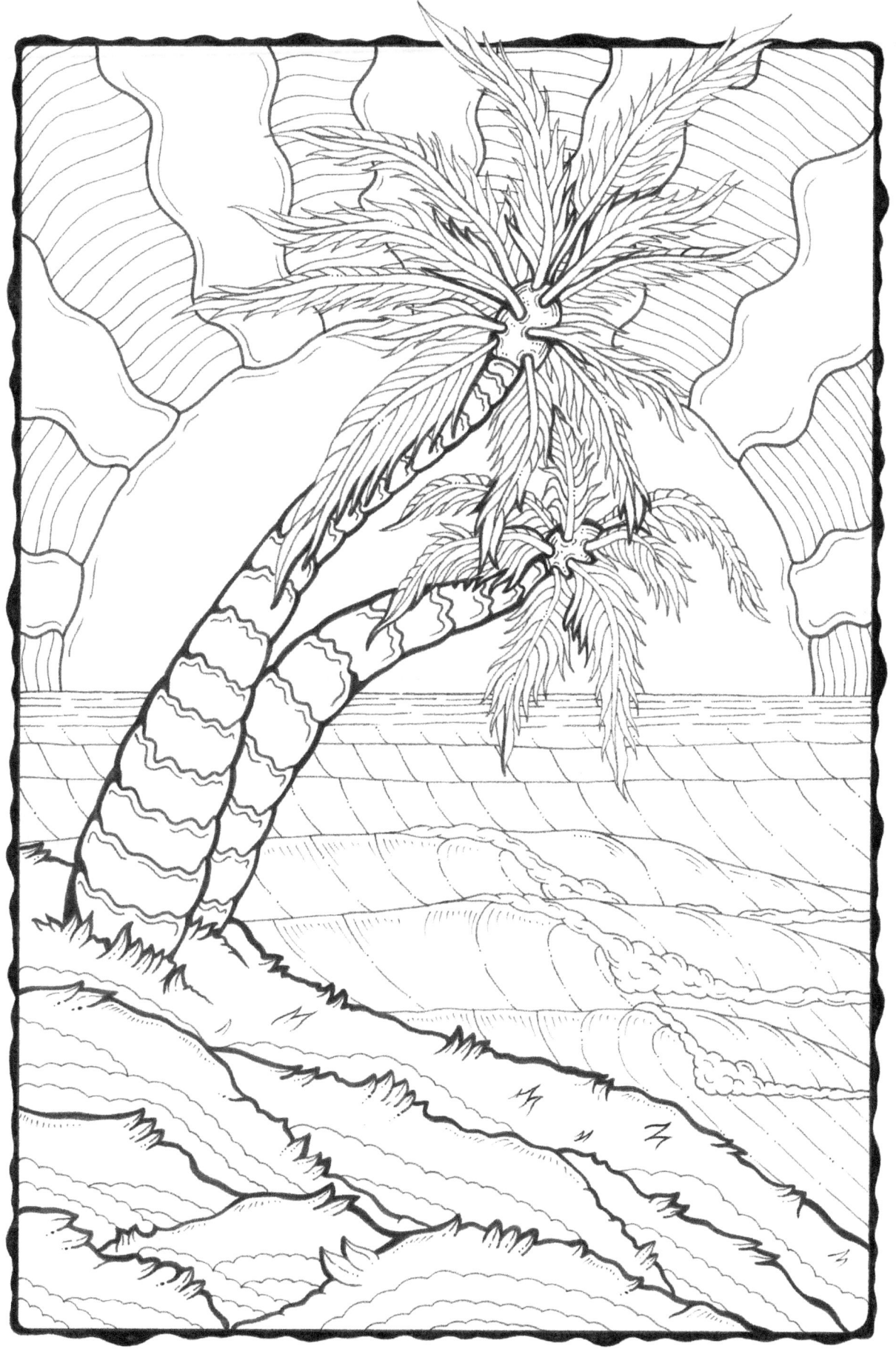

Turtley awesome!

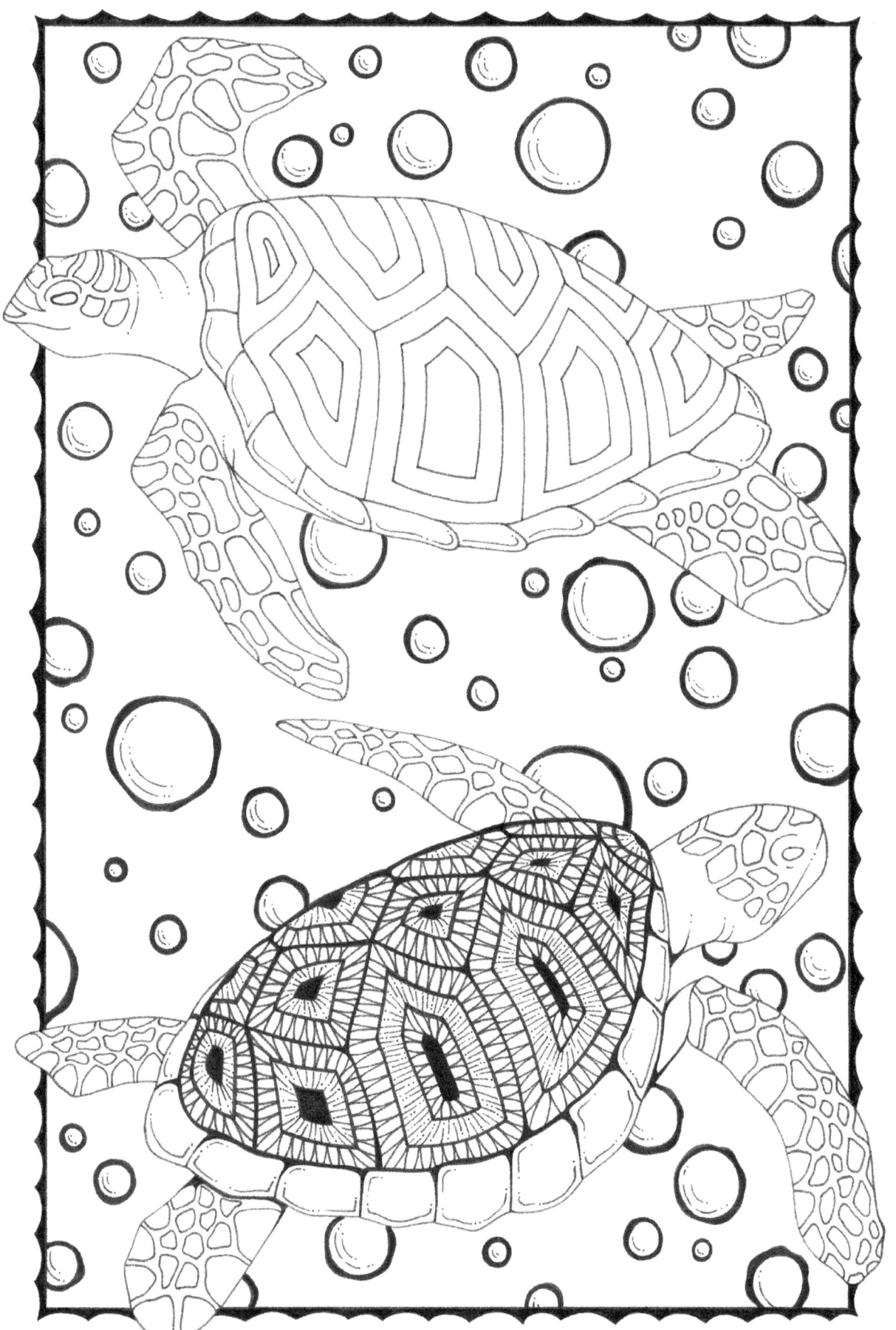

Even the sun needs some chill time

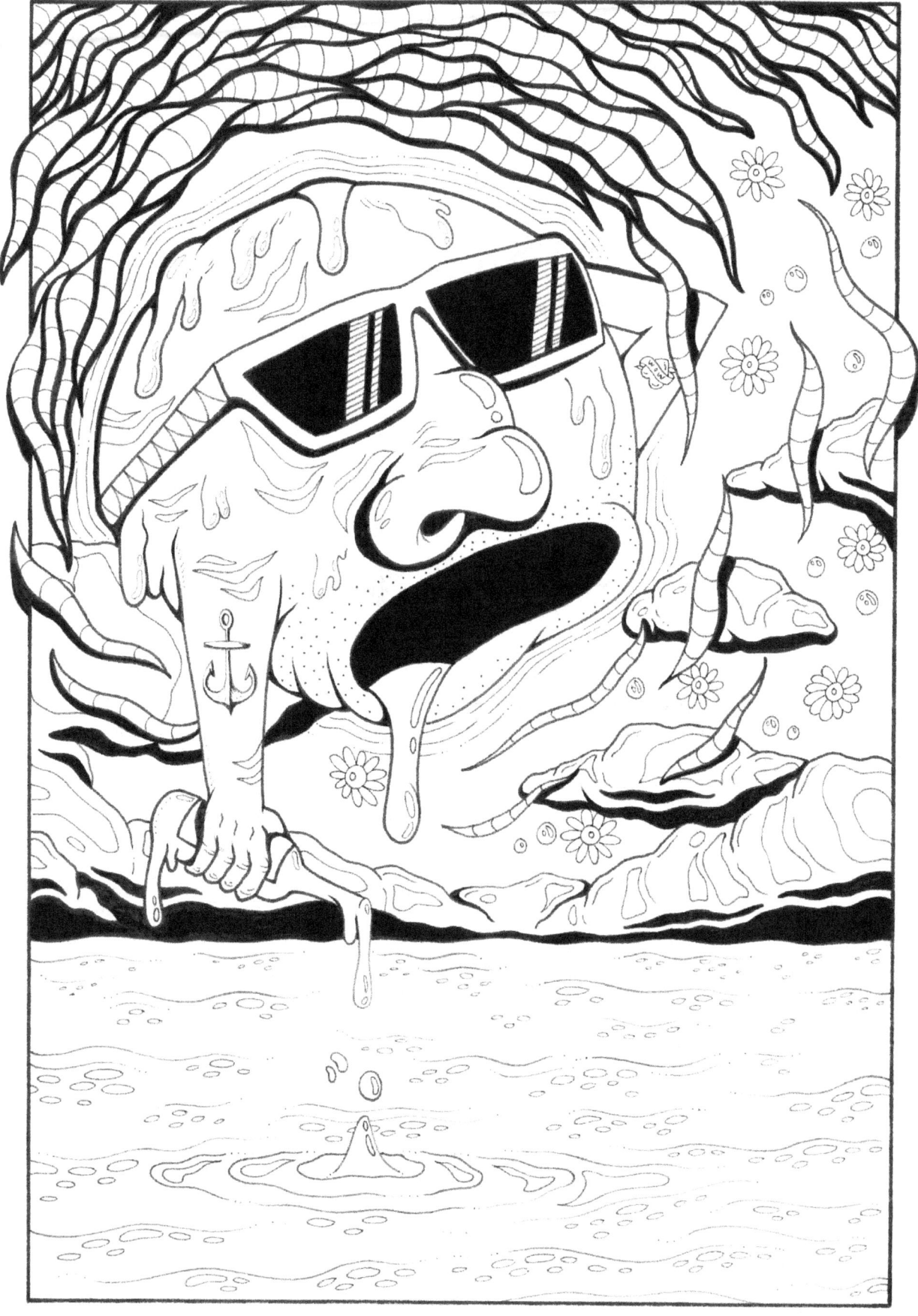

Thanks for coming along on this wild adventure!

I hope you've enjoyed the Beach Daze!

www.ingramcontent.com/pod-product-compliance
Lightning Source LLC
Chambersburg PA
CBHW081013170526
45158CB00010B/3029